THE DIVINE EYE

The Guru, Brahmgyan, and the Vision of God Within

दिव्य दृष्टि

गुरु, ब्रह्मज्ञान और ईश्वर के आंतरिक दर्शन

Anmol Setia

 This book is intended for educational and informational purposes only. The views and interpretations expressed in this work are those of the author and do not necessarily reflect those of any institution, organization, or individual.

Scriptural quotations appearing in this book are taken from traditional Hindu texts such as the Upanishads, the Bhagavad Gita, and other classical sources that are in the public domain. Translations are either the author's own or adapted from publicly available translations where appropriate. Every effort has been made to ensure the accuracy of the information contained in this book. However, the author shall not be liable for any loss or damages arising from the use of the information contained herein.

First Edition
Published in 2026

Author: Anmol Setia
Published by Anmol Setia
ISBN: 978-93-5890-540-3

The illustrations in this book are AI-assisted digital artworks created for symbolic and educational representation of spiritual concepts.

DEDICATION

At this most joyous and auspicious milestone—the completion of this humble work—I bow in profound reverence and dedicate this book at the sacred lotus feet of my revered Guru, ***Shri Ashutosh Maharaj Ji****. His divine vision, boundless grace, and illuminating guidance have been an eternal source of inspiration, shaping and sustaining me throughout this deeply transformative journey.*

I offer my heartfelt gratitude to ***Swami Mohanpuri Ji****, preacher at* **Divya Jyoti Jagrati Sansthan***, whose selfless support, wise counsel, and unwavering dedication have been invaluable in bringing this work to fruition. His readiness to guide me whenever I seek it has been a true blessing.*

I remain deeply indebted to my beloved family and cherished friends, whose sacrifices, steadfast patience, and constant encouragement have been my strength in moments of doubt and difficulty. Their faith in me has been my greatest support.

Finally, I extend my sincere appreciation to all who, directly or indirectly, contributed to the completion of this book. Their kindness, guidance, and goodwill shall forever remain etched in my heart.

With deepest humility and gratitude,
Anmol Setia

INTRODUCTION

The author, through his book, has attempted to present spiritual knowledge as contained in various ancient texts such as Upanishads, Ramcharitmanas, Bhagavad Gita, and other classical texts in a simple and structured form, connecting ancient knowledge with the current human quest for peace, truth, and happiness. The underlying theme of his work is a journey from information to realization, the need for a guru in the quest for Brahmgyan and achieving a direct perception of God.

This book is such that it promotes the idea of seeking the direct perception of God instead of depending on religious texts and rituals alone. It attempts to inspire readers to look for spiritual knowledge in different ancient texts, and spirituality is presented in the context of realization.

CONTENTS

PART - 1: ENGLISH

CHAPTER 1: GOD IS VISIBLE

God is Visible: A Divine Journey from Information to Realization

In human history, 'God' has always been the most discussed topic. Indian culture and the Upanishads declare that God is not just a matter of faith or a philosophical idea, He is a subject of direct 'Realization' (Sakshatkara). As Gurudev Shri Ashutosh Maharaj Ji often says, "If God exists, He must be visible." To understand this scientific journey of spirituality, the stories of 'Sanjaya' from the Mahabharata and 'Garuda' from the Ramayana are the best examples. Both had 'Information' (knowledge about God), but they lacked 'Realization' (experience of God). Sanjaya had 'Long distance Vision' to see the battlefield from far away and Garuda was the carrier of Lord Vishnu.

However, Sanjaya was only seeing outer scenes and Garuda was trapped in his own logical doubts. Both had sight, but they did not have the 'Divine Vision' needed to see God within their own hearts. This deep truth becomes clear in the story of Garuda's doubt. When Garuda saw Lord Ram bound by the 'Nagpash' (snake noose), he started doubting, "How can the Lord of the universe be captured by a snake?" To remove this darkness of ignorance, he was sent to Kakbhushundi Ji. Tulsidas Ji explains in the Ramcharitmanas, "Guru binu bhava nidhi tarai na koi..." which means that without a Guru, no one can cross the ocean of worldly sufferings, even if they are as powerful as Brahma or Shiva. Both Sanjaya and Garuda felt a deep emptiness inside. Sanjaya realized that when Arjuna closed his eyes, his face shone with divine peace. This restlessness led Sanjaya to Sage Shukdev Muni and Garuda to Kakbhushundi Ji.

Here, the importance of the human body is realized, it is a rare gift meant for turning 'inward' by seeking a Guru. Kakbhushundi Ji and Shukdev Muni introduced them to the secret of 'Bhakti Mani' (The Jewel of Devotion). True devotion is not just an outer ritual, it is a light that burns inside the heart. Tulsidas Ji describes it as, "Param prakas rup din rati, nahin kachu chahia dia ghrit bati" which means this inner light does not need any oil, wick, or lamp, it is the self-shining form of the soul. Just as clouds hide the sun, our thoughts and ignorance hide this light. Until a Perfect Guru opens the 'Divine Eye' (Third Eye), a person remains lost in the world of information. Real devotion starts only when the inner darkness is destroyed. An essential truth must be understood here: Real devotion (Bhakti) begins only after the eternal experience of God through 'Brahmgyan' (Divine Knowledge). Often, people think that doing Bhakti will lead them to God. But the scriptures say: How can you love (devote yourself to) someone you have never seen or met? Kakbhushundi Ji explained to Garuda that until the light of the "Bhakti Mani" appears within the heart, a person remains troubled by doubts and mental afflictions. When a person sees God within through the power of the Guru, their 'belief' turns into 'certainty'. This is the moment when a person 'knows' and then starts to 'believe'. This is the starting point of true, selfless devotion.

The method of 'Brahmgyan' is the scientific path that turns a seeker into a true devotee. When Shukdev Muni initiated Sanjaya and Kakbhushundi Ji initiated Garuda, a spiritual explosion happened inside them. The 'Universal Form' and the light of a thousand suns, which they had only described in words before, now appeared clearly inside them. When Garuda saw the true form of Ram within himself, all his doubts and mental pains vanished forever. This experience turned 'poison into nectar'. This inner vision (Insight) given by the Guru is far greater than any technology or outer vision. In conclusion, "God is visible" is not just a slogan, it is a living truth. Modern humans today are like Sanjaya filled with information from the internet and books—but lacking inner peace because they are only looking 'outside'. The real meaning of religion is 'to know' and knowing is only complete when we 'see'. With the grace of a Perfect Guru, a person can close their physical eyes and experience that Divine Light. When God is no longer just a thought but becomes a 'Visible Truth' inside us, only then is life successful and true devotion born.

CHATPER 2: BRAHMGYAN

Brahmgyan: From the Ashes of Ignorance to the Divine Awakening of Self Realization

The journey of spirituality is a movement from 'doubt' to 'truth'. In the Ramcharitmanas, the story of Mother Sati represents the conflict between the human ego and Divine reality. When Sati saw Lord Ram crying in the forest for Mother Sita, her logical mind doubted Him. She thought, "How can a God who is crying in grief be the Supreme Power?" Even after Lord Shiva explained it to her, she decided to test Ram by disguising herself as Sita. However, Lord Ram, being all knowing, recognized her immediately and addressed her as 'Mother' asking, "Where is Lord Shiva?" This story proves that God cannot be recognized through the outer eyes or by trickery. When Sati tried to understand Him through her limited mind, she failed.

Only when the veil of ego is removed can one see the truth, "Satin deekh jahan jahan chitvahi, tahan tahan Ramu sahit Shree rahi" which means wherever Sati looked, she saw Lord Ram and Goddess Lakshmi everywhere. Sati's act of taking the form of Sita was a spiritual mistake because she took the form of the Lord's wife. Because of this, Lord Shiva decided to end their worldly relationship as husband and wife, "Sati keenh Sita kar besha, Siv ur bhayu bishad bishesa" Afterward, Sati went to her father Daksha's sacrificial fire (Yagya). When she saw Shiva being insulted there, she could not bear it and sacrificed her body in the fire. This "burning" symbolizes the end of the 'old intellect' that sees God only as a human body. According to the Bhagavad Gita, the soul is eternal and only the body dies, "Vasansi jirnani yatha vihaya..." Sati's sacrifice was the foundation for her next birth as Parvati, where she would move from 'testing' God to 'realizing' Him. Born as Parvati, the daughter of the Himalayas, she performed intense penance. This time, she did not come to 'test' the Guru, but to be 'initiated' by Him. Lord Shiva, who is the Supreme Guru, provided her with 'Brahmgyan' (Divine Knowledge).

According to the Guru Gita, the Guru is the Supreme Reality, "Gurur Brahma, Gurur Vishnu, Gurur Devo Maheshwarah." Shiva opened her 'Divine Eye' (Third Eye) and showed her the same Light within herself that she was searching for outside in her previous birth. Shiva explained that Ram is not just the son of Dashrath, but the Eternal Light residing in everyone. The Guru Gita confirms this, "Ajñana timirandhasya jñanañjana shalakaya..." which means the Guru opens the eyes of those blinded by darkness with the needle of knowledge. It is vital to understand that 'Brahmgyan' is not just information, it is the science of the soul. When Parvati was initiated by Shiva, she realized that the Truth she was wandering for was actually located inside her, behind the 'Bhrumadhya' (center of the eyebrows). This was the moment when True Devotion (Bhakti) actually began. The Upanishads say, "Tadvigyanartham sa Gurumevabhigacchet" which means to know the truth, one must seek a Guru. Sati failed because she only had 'Information' but Parvati succeeded because she had 'Realization' given by the Guru.

Without the Divine Eye, it is impossible to see God's true form, just as Arjuna could not see the Universal Form until Krishna gave him Divine Vision. In conclusion, the journey from Sati to Parvati is the story of every seeker. As long as a human tries to 'test' God with the ego of the mind, they head toward 'ashes' (downfall). But when they surrender to a Perfect Guru (like Shiva) and awaken their 'Divine Eye' they see the true form of the Almighty. The 'Brahmgyan' received by the Guru's grace is the light that destroys the darkness of doubt. As the Guru Gita says, "Na Guroradhikam Tattvam" meaning there is no truth higher than the Guru. Only when the Light appears within can a person realize that God is not far away, but is eternally present inside us.

CHAPTER 3: FROM DEATH TO IMMORTALITY

From Death to Immortality: Nachiketa's Curiosity and the Realization of Brahmgyan

The essence of the Upanishads is the journey "from darkness to light" (Tamaso ma jyotirgamaya). In the Kathopanishad, the conversation between the young boy Nachiketa and Yamraj provides a scientific and spiritual map of this journey. When Nachiketa saw his father donating old, useless cows, his heart filled with a desire to know the absolute Truth. He reached the doorstep of Yamraj (the King of Death) and waited for three days without food or water. This patience symbolizes that the path to Brahmgyan (Divine Knowledge) opens only for a seeker who has true determination and detachment from worldly desires. To test him, Yamraj offered Nachiketa gold, a long life and all the pleasures of the world. However, Nachiketa rejected them saying, "Shvobhava martyasya yadantakaitat" meaning O Lord of Death, these pleasures are temporary and will end tomorrow.

Nachiketa's detachment proves that spiritual satisfaction cannot be achieved through information or material things. Seeing Nachiketa's worthiness, Yamraj granted him the 'Brahma Vidya' - the knowledge after which nothing else remains to be known. He explained that the soul is never born and never dies, "Na jayate mriyate va vipashchit." But knowing this is not just about words or philosophy. Yamraj introduced Nachiketa to the secret of the 'Divine Eye' (Third Eye). He explained that the Almighty resides within the heart in the form of a 'thumb sized' Light. Just as Sati needed Shiva and Parvati needed a Guru, Nachiketa required a 'Perfect Master' (Satguru) in the form of Yamraj to see this Light. A key scientific part of this story is the difference between the 'Shreya' (the path of ultimate good) and 'Preya' (the path of temporary pleasure). Yamraj says that the world offers two paths: one that feels good to the senses but leads to bondage and another that leads to the liberation of the soul.

A True Guru is one who shifts the seeker's focus from the outer world to the inner light. The principle of the Guru Gita is perfectly applied here: knowledge is impossible without a Guru. When Yamraj initiated Nachiketa into the eternal method of Brahmgyan, the 'Divine Light' appeared within him - a light that is beyond the sun, moon, or fire. The Upanishad says, "Tameva bhantamanubhati sarvam..." meaning when he shines, everything shines by his light, the entire universe is illuminated. It is important to clarify that the knowledge Nachiketa received was not just an idea, but a 'Permanent Realization'. Only after receiving the Divine Vision did Nachiketa experience that the same God who pervades the universe is present inside him as a spark of Light. His true devotion and peace began only after this direct 'Seeing' (Sakshatkara). Without this direct experience, the fear of death cannot vanish. Yamraj made it clear that spirituality is not magic, but a subtle science, often described as walking on a 'razor's edge', where the guidance of a Guru is mandatory.

The story of Nachiketa teaches us that no matter how learned we become, the mystery of death and the true form of God remain unsolved until we seek a Perfect Guru to awaken our 'Divine Eye'. Nachiketa achieved immortality through Brahmgyan. Even today, if a seeker wants to move from the world of information to the world of realization, they must find a Guru who can show them the Light. Only when we see the Divine Light within do we realize that we are not the body, but the eternal Soul. This is the ultimate goal of human life.

CHAPTER 4: "TAT TVAM ASI"

"Tat Tvam Asi": The Journey from the Ego of Information to the Truth of Realization

The real meaning of spirituality is not just memorizing scriptures, but seeing the 'Truth' within oneself. In the Chandogya Upanishad, the dialogue between Sage Aruni and his son Shvetaketu is a living proof of this. Shvetaketu studied all the Vedas and scriptures for twelve years, which made him arrogant about his knowledge. When he returned home, his father Aruni noticed that Shvetaketu had plenty of 'Information' but lacked 'Peace' and 'Realization'. His father asked a revolutionary question, "Shvetaketu! Have you known that 'Element' by knowing which the unheard becomes heard and the unknown becomes known?" Shvetaketu had no answer. This shows that outer education is just information, while Brahmgyan is the direct experience of the soul.

When Shvetaketu became curious, Sage Aruni explained using scientific examples. He told him that by knowing a single lump of clay, one knows everything made of clay. Similarly, by knowing that one Supreme God, the secret of the entire universe is revealed. The father asked Shvetaketu to put salt in water and return the next day. When he returned, the father said "Now, take out the salt." Shvetaketu could not see it because it had dissolved. The father explained that just as salt is present in every drop of water but is invisible, God is present in every atom of this body and universe but is hidden from physical eyes. To see Him, one needs the 'Divine Eye'.

As a Guru, the father gave Shvetaketu the ultimate teaching nine times, "Tat Tvam Asi" (You are That). This was not just a sentence, it was a process to connect Shvetaketu to the eternal Light within him. When Sage Aruni initiated Shvetaketu into Brahmgyan, Shvetaketu closed his eyes and realized that subtlest element. As the Guru Gita says, "Ajñana timirandhasya..." (The Guru removes the darkness of ignorance with the light of knowledge. The most important part of this story is that 'True Devotion' and 'Surrender' begin only after Brahmgyan. As long as Shvetaketu was just a scholar, he was arrogant. But when he received 'Divine Vision' from his Guru and saw himself as a part of that Supreme Light, his ego melted away. The Upanishad says, "Brahmavid Brahmaiva Bhavati" (The knower of Brahman becomes Brahman himself). This realization is the moment when a person's spiritual journey moves toward completion. Without seeing God directly, saying "I am That" is just information, but after seeing Him, it becomes a 'Realization'.

Shvetaketu's story is a great message for today's society. We have become like 'Sanjaya', filled with degrees and information, but we lack the inner sight. Until we seek a Perfect Guru and directly see God, who is present everywhere like salt in water, our knowledge remains incomplete. The real meaning of "Tat Tvam Asi" is only fulfilled when our 'Divine Eye' is opened by the Guru's grace and we see our soul merging with the Supreme. This realization is the ultimate goal of human life.

CHAPTER 5: THE SEARCH FOR ETERNAL TRUTH

The Search for Eternal Truth: From Darkness to Divine Realization

The spiritual journey of humanity has always been from the 'outside' to the 'inside'. Indian scriptures like the Upanishads and Ramcharitmanas prove that God is not just a topic of discussion or faith, but a direct 'Experience'. This science of spirituality explains that as long as humans see the world through physical eyes, they remain in doubt. But when a Perfect Guru opens the 'Divine Eye' (Third Eye), one can see the Truth directly. The stories of Sati becoming Parvati, Nachiketa's dialogue with Yamraj and Shvetaketu's education from Sage Aruni all prove one thing, "God is visible and the Divine Vision given by a Guru is mandatory to see Him."

1. From Sati to Parvati: From Logic to Devotion

The story of Sati represents the ego of the human mind. When she saw Lord Ram crying for Sita, her 'information based' mind doubted His divinity. She tested Him by disguising herself as Sita, which was a mistake. After her death and rebirth as Parvati, she chose 'penance' and 'initiation' instead of 'testing'. When Lord Shiva, as her Guru, gave her 'Brahmgyan' and awakened the Light within her, she realized that Ram is the eternal God, not just a human. The Guru Gita says, "Ajñana timirandhasya..." meaning the Guru opens the eyes of those blinded by ignorance using the light of knowledge.

2. Nachiketa's Detachment: Finding Immortality

In the Kathopanishad, Nachiketa teaches us that worldly pleasures cannot give soul satisfaction. Yamraj offered him all the wealth and pleasures of heaven, but Nachiketa stayed firm on his question, "I want the knowledge that removes the fear of death." Yamraj, acting as a Perfect Guru, showed him the Divine Light residing within his heart. He explained that God is not found through big words or intelligence, but through 'Direct Experience' given by a Guru. This Brahmgyan was not just a thought, it was a realization of Light that turned the fear of death into a celebration.

3. Shvetaketu and 'Tat Tvam Asi': Beyond Information

In the Chandogya Upanishad, Shvetaketu was proud of his scriptural knowledge. His father and Guru, Sage Aruni, realized that this was just 'Information' not 'Peace'. Using the example of salt in water, Aruni explained that God is present in the body like salt in water - invisible to the eyes but present everywhere. When Aruni gave him the teaching of "Tat Tvam Asi" (You are That), it was a spiritual process that connected Shvetaketu to the eternal Light within. Only after this realization did Shvetaketu's ego melt and true devotion began.

4. The Science of Brahmgyan and the Need for a Guru

In all three stories, one thing is common that no one saw the Truth without a Guru. The Ramcharitmanas says, "Guru binu bhava nidhi tarai na koi..." (No one can cross the ocean of life without a Guru). A Guru is like a scientist who activates the Third Eye where the soul meets God. This is not magic, but the science of the soul. True devotion begins only after 'Seeing' (Realization). Without this direct experience, devotion is just a mental imagination.

We can come to the conclusion that realization is the perfection of life. The journeys of Sati, Nachiketa and Shvetaketu teach us that religion is not just about rituals or reading books, it is about 'Knowing Thyself'. Today, Gurudev Shri Ashutosh Maharaj Ji is reviving this same method of 'Brahmgyan'. When God is seen 'within', doubts vanish, the fear of death ends and ego is destroyed. This Divine Vision is the bridge from the world of information to the world of realization. The day a person sees that "Light of a thousand suns" within, their spiritual journey becomes successful.

CHAPTER 6: DUALISM TO DIVINE UNITY

Two Birds and One Tree: The Journey from Dualism to Divine Unity

The greatest mystery of spirituality is understanding who we are and our relationship with the Supreme Power. In the Mundaka Upanishad, Sage Angira explains this to his disciple Shaunaka through a beautiful scientific metaphor. He says that on the same tree (the body), two birds with beautiful wings (the Soul and God) live together as friends, "Dva suparna sayuja sakhaya..." One bird (the Soul/Jiva) eats the fruits of the tree (actions and results) while the other bird (God) simply watches as a witness without eating anything. This story proves that even though we are very close to God, we feel separate from Him due to ignorance.

The scientific analysis of this story is that as long as the soul (the bird) is busy eating the sweet and bitter fruits of the world, it remains troubled and restless. It is like 'Sanjaya', who was lost in outer sights. According to the Mundaka Upanishad, the soul's suffering ends only when it turns its gaze away from the fruits and looks toward its 'Friend' - the witness bird (God). But this shift in vision only happens when a person finds a 'Perfect Guru' who can teach them that they are not slaves to their actions, but a part of the Supreme Brahman.

The Guru's role is decisive here. The Upanishad says that to know that Eternal Truth, one must seek a Guru with humility - "Tadvigyanartham sa Gurumevabhigacchet." Just as Sati needed Shiva and Nachiketa needed Yamraj, Shaunaka took initiation from Sage Angira. When the Guru awakened Shaunaka's 'Divine Eye' (Third Eye) through the method of Brahmgyan, he realized that the 'Witness Bird' was none other than the Divine Light sitting inside his own heart. As the Guru Gita says, the Guru is the light that cuts the bonds of attachment.

True devotion begins only after this eternal experience of Brahmgyan. When a seeker sees the Divine Light within, the knots of the heart are opened and all doubts are destroyed - "Bhidyate Hridaya granthish..." The Mundaka Upanishad clarifies that this knowledge is not gained through logic or intelligence, but through direct 'Realization' (Sakshatkara). After receiving the Divine Vision, a person experiences that they are not the suffering bird eating the fruits, but the eternal, free consciousness.

This story from the Mundaka Upanishad is both a warning and a solution for the modern human. We are so busy "eating the fruits" of information and worldly life that we have forgotten the 'Witnessing God' within us. Until we seek a Perfect Guru and see the Divine Light inside, we will remain trapped in the cycle of pleasure and pain. Brahmgyan is the Divine Eye that makes us realize that God is not far away, but is shining within our own heart. Realization is the ultimate truth that gives meaning and perfection to human life.

CHAPTER 7: PRASHNA UPANISHAD

Prashna Upanishad and Ajapa Japa: From the Mystery of Breath to the Realization of Om

What is the core of human life? In the Prashna Upanishad, Sage Pippalada teaches six seekers about the science of 'Prana' (Life force) and 'Om'. He explains that the root of the universe is Prana. However, the deepest spiritual truth is that a constant chant is happening inside us, known as 'Ajapa Japa'. This is a chant that is not done with the tongue, it happens naturally with every breath. Sage Pippalada teaches that the supreme form of 'Om' is not just something to read or hear, but something to 'Experience' in the inner world.

The scientific side of this story is that 'Ajapa Japa' (the natural rhythm of breath) happens 24 hours a day in every human, but we cannot hear it because of ignorance. Just as Sage Pippalada initiated his disciples after a year of discipline, Gurudev Shri Ashutosh Maharaj Ji explains that without 'Brahmgyan' and the Guru's grace, we cannot hear this subtle inner sound (Anahad Naad). The Guru is the scientist who shifts our consciousness from outer noise to the inner vibration of 'Om'.

The Guru’s role is essential in realizing the true form of 'Om'. Sage Pippalada teaches that Om is not just a letter, it is the sound of the Divine. When a Perfect Guru awakens the

'Divine Eye' and the inner ears of a seeker, they realize that 'Ajapa Japa' is the real practice. This chant is revealed in the inner world only through the Guru's grace. Without initiation, a person only repeats words (Information) but after initiation, they merge into that inner music (Realization).

The most important teaching of this Upanishad is that God is right here, inside the body— "Ihaiva antah sharire sa purusho..." When the Guru gives Brahmgyan, the disciple realizes that the sound and light of Om are not coming from outside, but are the very source of their own life. Through Ajapa Japa, the seeker's soul merges into the Great Divine Power. This direct realization is 'Immortality'.

In conclusion, the Prashna Upanishad teaches us not to be just collectors of information like 'Sanjaya'. The real truth is 'Ajapa Japa' which is known only within the inner world through the Guru's grace. When the Guru's power opens the 'Divine Eye' and the inner sound of Om begins to ring, only then do all life's questions end. This direct seeing is the ultimate truth that gives perfection and peace to human life.

CHAPTER 8: AITAREYA UPANISHAD

Aitareya Upanishad: From the Mystery of Creation to the Realization of 'Prajnanam Brahma'

What existed at the beginning of creation? Who created this body and the universe? The Aitareya Upanishad answers these questions by stating that in the beginning, only the 'Atman' (Soul) existed. It created the worlds and then entered the bodies itself. The most revolutionary truth of this Upanishad is that God is not sitting in a distant heaven, He has entered our body through the crown of the head. Sage Aitareya explains that the same 'Brahman' is the one seeing through our eyes, hearing through our ears and thinking through our minds.

The Mahavakya (Great Saying) of this Upanishad is "Prajnanam Brahma" (Consciousness is Brahman). But this consciousness cannot be realized just by reading or hearing (Information). Just as Sanjaya could see the scenes of the Mahabharata but could not 'feel' the inner peace, a common person hears about God but does not 'know' Him. Sage Aitareya clarifies that the realization of that 'Prajnan' (Consciousness) is possible only through Brahmgyan given by a Guru. When the 'Divine Eye' is opened by the Guru's grace, a person realizes they are not the body, but the vast conscious power that supports the entire universe.

A hidden secret of spirituality is that God's presence is constantly within us in the form of 'Ajapa Japa' and 'Anahad Naad' (Inner Sound). Gurudev Shri Ashutosh Maharaj Ji often says that the Guru is the power who gathers our scattered consciousness and connects it to the 'Great Light' within. According to the Aitareya Upanishad, when a seeker seeks shelter in a Guru, they realize that the 'Light' inside is the source of the entire universe. Without the Guru's grace, a person wanders in the illusions of dreams and waking life, but the Guru leads them to the 'Turiya' (Supreme Consciousness) state.

The main message of this Upanishad is that once a soul 'sees' its true self, it becomes free from the cycle of birth and death. Just as Nachiketa learned from Yamraj and Shvetaketu from Aruni, the seeker of Sage Aitareya experiences that 'Prajnan' is the only truth. When 'Ajapa Japa' and Divine Light appear within through the Guru's grace, the seeker realizes their complete self. This is the moment when 'True Devotion' begins because now the devotee does not just believe in God but sees Him directly.

In conclusion, the Aitareya Upanishad shows us the path to rise above Sanjaya's informative vision and realize 'Prajnan' (Consciousness). Seeing God is not a fantasy, it is a living truth possible through the 'Divine Vision' given by a Guru. When a person recognizes that eternal consciousness within, only then is the purpose of life fulfilled. Realization is the ultimate peace that grants immortality to a human being.

CHAPTER 9: KENA UPANISHAD

Kena Upanishad: From the Driver of the Mind to the Realization of 'Brahman'

"By whom is the mind directed to fall on its objects? Who directs the first breath (Prana) to move? Who gives the power to eyes and ears?" The Kena Upanishad starts with these fundamental questions (Kena = By whom). The Sage explains that That which cannot be seen by eyes, but by which the eyes see, That which cannot be thought by the mind, but by which the mind thinks—That alone is 'Brahman'. This Upanishad makes it clear that God is not an external object to be caught by our senses, but the very source of our consciousness.

The deepest truth of this Upanishad is that the person who claims they "know" Brahman (intellectually) actually does not know Him. This is because Brahman is not a subject of 'Information' but of 'Realization'. The Sage says that God is known only by the one who sees Him directly in every experience (Pratibodha). Just as 'Sanjaya' had information about the battlefield but lacked the divine experience of Arjuna, the Sage clarifies that the opening of the 'Divine Eye' is possible only through a Guru. Only then can we see the power that is vibrating within us as 'Ajapa Japa' and 'Prana'.

To explain the necessity of a Guru, there is a story of 'Yaksha and the Devas' in this Upanishad. When Agni (Fire),

Vayu (Wind) and Indra became arrogant about their powers, Brahman appeared as a 'Yaksha' (a mysterious Spirit). Agni could not burn a blade of grass and Vayu could not blow it away. Then Indra realized that all their powers were actually gifts from 'Brahman'. At that moment, 'Uma' (Divine Knowledge/Guru Power) appeared and gave Indra the true knowledge of Brahman. This story proves that without Guru Power, even great powers and bookish knowledge are useless. The Guru is the guide who makes us realize that the Light within us is the foundation of the universe.

The science of spirituality says that just as a flash of lightning happens (Vidyuto vyadyutada), the light of Brahman suddenly appears in the seeker's inner world by the Guru's grace. 'True Devotion' begins only after this direct experience. Gurudev Shri Ashutosh Maharaj Ji often discusses this method - that when a Guru gives Brahmgyan, a person closes their eyes and directly sees that Supreme Light within. According to the Kena Upanishad, if one realizes this Truth in this very life, their life is successful otherwise there is great loss.

The Kena Upanishad shows us the path to rise above Sanjaya's superficial vision and realize the 'Root Power' that is the basis of our existence. Seeing God within through the 'Divine Vision' given by a Guru, rather than just using logic, is the real goal of religion. When the experience of 'Ajapa Japa' and Divine Light happens within, only then does a person become free from ego and achieve perfect peace. Realization is the nectar that grants immortality to the soul.

CHAPTER 10: BRIHADARANYAKA UPANISHAD

Brihadaranyaka Upanishad: From the Darkness of Ignorance to the Light of the Soul

"Tamaso ma jyotirgamaya" (Lead me from darkness to light). This famous prayer from the Brihadaranyaka Upanishad is the entire essence of spirituality. In this Upanishad, Sage Yajnavalkya provides King Janaka and his wife Maitreyi with the knowledge that frees a human from all worldly bonds. The Sage explains that everything we love in this world is actually loved because of the 'Atman' (Soul) that resides within us.

A great scientific dialogue in this Upanishad takes place between King Janaka and Sage Yajnavalkya regarding 'Light'. King Janaka asks, "O Sage! When the sun sets, the moon goes down and the fire is extinguished, by what light does a human function?" The Sage replies, "Then Sound is his light." Janaka asks further, "And when sound also becomes silent, by what light does he move?" Then Yajnavalkya says, "Atmaiva asya jyotir bhavati" (The Soul itself becomes his light). This proves that behind our physical eyes, there is another Light that cannot be seen without the 'Divine Eye'.

Sage Yajnavalkya explains that this Light of the Soul is 'Brahman' and realizing it is impossible without the grace of a Guru. The Mahavakya of this Upanishad is "Aham

Brahmasmi" (I am Brahman). But this is not just something to say (Information). Just as 'Sanjaya' was only describing outer events, an ordinary person only says "I am Brahman" in words. Real 'Realization' happens when a Guru gives the initiation of 'Brahmgyan'. Through the Guru's power, when 'Ajapa Japa' and 'Anahad Naad' ring within, the seeker directly experiences that the same Light in the sun and moon is also burning inside them.

The Upanishad emphasizes the necessity of a Guru by saying that the Soul is "Drashtavyah" (to be seen). Here, 'to be seen' means 'Direct Realization'. Gurudev Shri Ashutosh Maharaj Ji often highlights this Vedic method - that God is not a fantasy, but a 'Vision' to be seen within. When a person sees that eternal Light inside by the Guru's grace, only then does their 'True Devotion' begin. Then they realize they are not the body, but a part of the Divine.

The Brihadaranyaka Upanishad shows us the path to rise above Sanjaya's limited informative vision and see the 'Self Light' that never sets. Seeing God within is the real meaning of moving from darkness to light. When we directly see the truth of 'Aham Brahmasmi' through the 'Divine Vision' given by a Guru, only then does the fear of death vanish. Realization is the nectar that frees the soul from all sufferings and grants perfection.

CHAPTER 11: MANDUKYA UPANISHAD

Mandukya Upanishad: From the Secrets of Om to the Realization of 'Turiya'

At what levels does human consciousness function? Mandukya Upanishad answers this through a scientific analysis of 'Om' (AUM). The Sages declare that this entire universe is Om. Whatever has passed, what is present and what will be in the future, is all Omkara. But Om is not just a word, it is a journey of consciousness that leads beyond waking, dreaming and deep sleep to the state of 'Turiya' (The Fourth State).

The Mahavakya of this Upanishad is "Ayamatma Brahma" (This Atman/Soul is Brahman). The Sage explains that the soul has four stages. The first is the waking state, the second is the dream state, the third is deep sleep. But the fourth stage, called 'Turiya' is the true nature of the soul. This 'Turiya' state is that peaceful and non-dual element after which nothing more remains to be achieved.

The Sage clarifies that realizing this 'Turiya' state is not possible through 'Information' alone. Just as 'Sanjaya' was only seeing events of the waking world, Arjuna experienced the supreme light of Turiya. To reach this state, the role of a Guru is mandatory. The Guru is the scientist who, through the method of Brahmgyan, lifts the seeker's consciousness above the body and mind to connect it with the Supreme Element. When 'Ajapa Japa' and 'Divine Light' appear within by the Guru's grace, the seeker can 'see' the true formless nature of Om.

Gurudev Shri Ashutosh Maharaj Ji often discusses this fourth state (Turiya), stating it is not a mental fantasy but a 'Realization'. When the Guru opens the 'Divine Eye', a person experiences that the inner sound of Om (Anahad Naad) is constantly ringing within them. This is the moment when 'Ayamatma Brahma' becomes a living experience. 'True Devotion' starts only after this vision, as the devotee now experiences God as their own soul.

The Mandukya Upanishad teaches us not to remain just 'Sanjayas' of the waking world but to become seers of 'Turiya' through a Guru. Seeing God within is the end of all suffering. When we realize that peaceful and non-dual form of Omkara through the 'Divine Vision' given by a Guru, only then is the purpose of life fulfilled. Realization is the nectar that grants immortality and supreme peace.

CHAPTER 12: TAITTIRIYA UPANISHAD

Taittiriya Upanishad: From the Five Sheaths to the Realization of 'Bliss'

What is the true nature of a human being? Is it just a body of flesh and bones? The Taittiriya Upanishad explains this through the science of 'Pancha Kosha' (Five Sheaths). The Sage teaches that the Soul is hidden behind five layers: the physical body, energy, mind, intellect and finally, Anandamaya (the layer of Bliss). Everyone is looking for happiness, but that happiness is limited to the outer layers. Sage Varuna teaches his son Bhrigu that "Ananda" (Bliss) is Brahman, because everything is born from bliss and merges back into it.

The main declaration of this Upanishad is "Raso Vai Sah" (God is Bliss Himself). But this bliss cannot be experienced through senses or information. Just as 'Sanjaya' had all the information about the war but was still sad, an ordinary person stays trapped in the layers of body and mind. On the other hand, Arjuna, by Krishna's grace, crossed these layers and realized the 'Blissful' Brahman. The Sage makes it clear that only by seeking a Guru can one cross these layers and see the inner Light.

The role of the Guru is essential because realizing Brahman is not a fantasy. When a Guru gives the initiation of

Brahmgyan, he leads the seeker from the intellect to the Soul. The Guru is the power who connects the seeker to the 'Ajapa Japa' happening within and leads them to the 'Heart Cave' where there is only Divine Light. Gurudev Shri Ashutosh Maharaj Ji explains that when the Guru opens the 'Divine Eye', a person realizes that the peace they were searching for outside is actually present at their own center as 'Light'.

Another important truth of this Upanishad is, "Yato vacho nivartante..." (Where words and mind return from, without reaching it). This means God is not a subject of logic or words, but of direct 'Seeing'. When the 'Anahad Naad' (Inner Sound) rings and Divine Light appears by the Guru's grace, the seeker becomes free from fear. This is where 'True Devotion' begins, as the devotee now sees the Bliss directly inside.

The Taittiriya Upanishad teaches us not to be 'Sanjayas' trapped in the layers of body and mind, but to be seekers of 'Bliss' like Bhrigu. Seeing God is the supreme bliss of life. When we experience that 'God as Bliss' through the 'Divine Vision' given by a Guru, only then do all life's struggles end. Realization is the nectar that gives ultimate satisfaction and eternal happiness to a human being.

CHAPTER 13: ISHA UPANISHAD

Isha Upanishad: Realizing the 'Light' Pervading Every Atom of the Universe

Does God live somewhere far away in the sky? The Isha Upanishad clears this doubt in its very first verse, "Ishavasyam idam sarvam..." (Everything in this moving universe is pervaded by God). This Upanishad teaches that the world we see is not just physical matter, it is an expansion of the Supreme Consciousness. However, the question remains: If God is everywhere, why can't we see Him?

The Sage answers that the face of Truth is covered by a 'Golden Lid' (Hiranmaya Patra) : "Hiranmayena patrena satyasyapihitam mukham." This golden lid represents our ego and the attractions of the world. Just as 'Sanjaya' had all the information and wealth of the war but could not see Krishna's cosmic form due to the lid of attachment, an ordinary person stays blind to the Truth. The Sage prays, "O Lord! Remove that lid so I may see the Truth" This proves that 'Seeing' God is the ultimate goal of spirituality.

In this Upanishad, the role of a Guru is like the 'Sun' that removes the veil of ignorance. The Guru is the guide who, through Brahmgyan, shows the seeker that transcendental Light. The Sage says, "Yatte rupam kalyanatamam tatte pashyami" (O Sun! Withdraw your rays so that I may see your most auspicious form). Here, the word 'Pashyami' (I see) is proof of direct realization. When the 'Ajapa Japa' is activated by the Guru's grace and the 'Divine Eye' opens, the seeker experiences that the Power in the Sun is the same Power within them (So'ham asmi).

The science of spirituality says that one who balances Vidya (Divine Knowledge) and Avidya (Worldly Duties) crosses death and attains immortality. Gurudev Shri Ashutosh Maharaj Ji explains that believing in God is just 'Information' but seeing Him in every atom is 'Realization'. When the 'Anahad Naad' rings within through the Guru's power, the seeker realizes that God is shining in every pore of their body. This is where 'True Devotion' begins.

The Isha Upanishad frees us from Sanjaya's limited vision and gives us the Divine Vision of a Sage. Seeing God not as separate from the world, but within every atom of it, is the real meaning of religion. When we remove the 'Golden Lid' and see the Truth inside through the 'Divine Vision' given by a Guru, only then is the purpose of life fulfilled. Realization is the nectar that frees the soul from all bonds and grants eternal peace.

CHAPTER 14: KAUSHITAKI UPANISHAD

Kaushitaki Upanishad: From Prana to Prajna and the Realization of Brahman

Which power is the greatest in the human body? The Kaushitaki Upanishad answers this through a dialogue between King Pratardana and Indra. Indra declares, "Prano asmi prajnatma" (I am Prana and I am the Divine Intelligence/Prajna). This Upanishad clarifies that life is not just about breathing, it is about experiencing the consciousness that drives the breath. The Sages explain that as long as 'Prana' is in the body, there is life and that Prana is truly 'Brahman'.

The deepest scientific aspect of this Upanishad is that 'Prana' (Life force) and 'Prajna' (Consciousness) are one and the same. Just as 'Sanjaya' had the power to see but lacked the 'Divine Prajna' to understand Krishna's essence, an ordinary person remains blind to the source of life. The Sage says that speech, sight, hearing and mind are all subordinate to Prana. This proves there is a 'Centre' within us where everything merges. Knowing that centre is Brahmgyan.

The role of a Guru is to awaken this 'Prajna'. The Guru is the scientist who teaches the disciple, "Do not seek to know speech, know the Speaker, do not seek to know the form, know the Seer" Realizing this 'Seer' is only possible through a Guru's grace. When the Guru grants the 'Divine Eye', the sound of 'Ajapa Japa' resonates within and the seeker experiences that their life force is a part of the 'Supreme Life force' (God).

The science of spirituality says that just as the spokes of a wheel are fixed to the hub, all elements of existence are fixed to 'Prajna' and 'Prana'. Gurudev Shri Ashutosh Maharaj Ji often discusses this inner balance - that when the Guru opens the inner door through Brahmgyan, a person directly sees the Divine Light. According to the Kaushitaki Upanishad, one who 'sees' this Truth becomes free from all sins and attains the blissful realm. This is where 'True Devotion' begins.

The Kaushitaki Upanishad leads us above Sanjaya's external vision to the realization of 'Prajna'. Seeing God not just in the movement of breath but as the 'Divine Consciousness' behind it is the real goal of religion. When we realize that blissful, ageless and immortal element through the 'Divine Vision' given by a Guru, only then is the purpose of life fulfilled. Realization is the divine experience that frees a human from worldly bonds and grants eternal peace.

CHAPTER 15: MAHANARAYANA UPANISHAD

Mahanarayana Upanishad: Realizing the 'Divine Light' Within the Heart Lotus

Where is the center of the universe? Where does that Supreme Power reside, described as "smaller than the smallest and greater than the greatest"? The Mahanarayana Upanishad reveals that God is not in the sky but resides within the 'Heart Lotus' (Dahara Pundarika) of a human. The Sages explain that within the center of the body, there is a subtle space and within that space, one finds the Light that illuminates everything.

The most scientific verse of this Upanishad describes the appearance of this inner Light, "Nila toyada madhyastha vidyullekheva Bhasvara." This means the Light shines like a streak of lightning in the middle of dark blue clouds. Just as 'Sanjaya' could only see the external battlefield, an ordinary person only knows the physical heart. But the Sage clarifies that when the 'Divine Eye' is opened through Brahmgyan given by a Guru, the seeker directly experiences that lightning like brilliant Light. This Light is 'Narayana', the true form of the Soul.

The Upanishad emphasizes that without 'Initiation' and 'Guru's Grace', this subtle path cannot be known. The Guru is the scientist who guides the life force and connects the seeker to that inner Light through 'Ajapa Japa'. According to the Mahanarayana Upanishad, one who sees this Light attains the highest state. Gurudev Shri Ashutosh Maharaj Ji proves this Vedic method today - that when the Guru awakens the 'Third Eye', a person sees that golden radiance within their own closed eyes.

The science of spirituality says that this realization is 'Immortality'. When the 'Anahad Naad' rings within and the Divine Light appears, the seeker realizes, "So'ham asmi" (I am That). This is where 'True Devotion' begins. The devotee no longer just imagines God but sees Him directly within their own self. After this vision, the ego is destroyed and the person achieves perfect peace.

The Mahanarayana Upanishad leads us beyond Sanjaya's limited information to the vision of the 'Heart Light' that shines like a flash of lightning. Searching for God only in logic is useless, seeing Him through the 'Divine Vision' given by a Guru within the Heart Lotus is the real goal of religion. When the Guru's power unites 'Ajapa Japa' and Divine Light within, the purpose of life is fulfilled. Realization is the ultimate truth that grants immortality and eternal bliss.

CHAPTER 16: GURU'S GRACE ON KING PRAKSHIT

The Supreme State of Parikshit: From Hearing to Realization via Guru's Grace

On the seventh day of the Srimad Bhagavatam, a divine miracle took place. The revered saint Dongre Ji Maharaj explains that after seven days of preaching, Sage Shukadeva placed his hand on King Parikshit's head and commanded, "O King! Now close your eyes and fix your attention on the Divine Light that I am about to manifest within you."

This moment is a testament to the science of 'Shaktipat' (Transmission of Power). For Parikshit, this was the transition from 'Information' to 'Realization'. Just as Sanjaya had limited vision, Shukadeva gave Parikshit the 'Inner Vision' to see himself as a 'Beaming Soul' separate from the body. Through the Guru's touch, the 'Ajapa Japa' and the 'Divine Light' were activated within him.

Dongre Ji Maharaj highlights that until a Guru opens the inner door, God remains just a story. Shukadeva told the story for seven days to purify Parikshit's mind and finally, through his touch, he revealed the Truth. When Parikshit saw that 'Sun like Light' within, the fear of the serpent Takshaka vanished. He realized that death is just like changing clothes, while the Soul is eternal light.

Parikshit's story teaches us that the spiritual journey ends not with 'hearing' but with 'seeing'. Only the 'Divine Vision' given by a Guru can destroy the fear of death. Realization is the ultimate truth that merges the soul with the Divine and grants immortality.

CHAPTER 17: JOURNEY OF SAGE SHUKADEVA

Sage Shukadeva: The Realized Master and the Science of Brahmgyan

Sage Shukadeva is the supreme hero of the Srimad Bhagavat Purana and a symbol of the highest spiritual state. However, the greatest secret of his life is that even though he was enlightened from birth, he had to seek a 'Living Guru' (King Janaka) for guidance. Though he was the son of Sage Ved Vyasa and possessed knowledge since he was in the womb, he was sent to King Janaka to achieve perfection. This event proves that the actual realization of 'Brahmgyan' is possible only in the presence of a 'Living Realized Master'.

1. Initiation from King Janaka: The Ideal of Guru Disciple Tradition

Shukadeva had the knowledge of scriptures, but to turn that knowledge into 'Direct Realization' and 'Stability', he had to go to King Janaka. King Janaka tested him and finally granted him the secret of the 'Divine Eye' (Third Eye), through which Shukadeva's consciousness merged completely into Brahman. From here, he learned how to live in the world while being 'Videha' (free from body consciousness). Using this same power, he later became the Guru of King Parikshit. According to Dongre Ji Maharaj, the knowledge that Shukadeva received from Janaka was the same power he transferred to Parikshit.

2. Information vs. Realization: The True Duty of a Guru

There are two levels of knowledge in the world - 'Paroksha' (Information) and 'Aparoksha' (Realization). King Parikshit had no lack of information at the time of his death, but it did not help him. Shukadeva proved that the true duty of a Guru is not just to speak words, but to manifest the 'Light within'. Explaining this, Dongre Ji Maharaj says that after seven days of preaching, Shukadeva placed his hand on Parikshit's head and said, "O King! Now close your eyes and focus your attention on the Light that I am going to manifest inside you."

3. The Science of Brahmgyan and Shaktipat

Shukadeva gave Parikshit the secret of 'Ajapa Japa' which continues constantly with every breath. The Guru placing his hand on the disciple's head is actually the process of 'Shaktipat' (Transmission of Power). Through this power, the 'Anahad Naad' rings inside the disciple and the 'Divine Light' is seen. Shukadeva taught Parikshit how to merge his consciousness into that inner 'Light'. Here, 'Sanjaya' (the one who only gives information) ends and the 'Seer' (the one who realizes) awakens.

4. True Devotion: The Journey After Realization

Shukadeva proved that 'True Devotion' begins only after 'Darshan' (Seeing). Until the Guru opens the inner door, God remains just an 'imagination'. With the power of 'Brahmgyan' received from King Janaka, Shukadeva made Parikshit realize that he is not the body, but the Soul itself. Parikshit himself admitted that he no longer feared death because he had directly seen the 'Imperishable Light' within himself.

The life of Shukadeva teaches us that if a great soul like him needed a Guru (Janaka), then an ordinary human cannot know Brahman without a Master. Believing in God is just 'Information', but 'Seeing' Him (Realization) is true knowledge. This 'Divine Vision' given by the Guru is the ultimate truth that destroys the darkness of death and gives meaning to life.

CHAPTER 18: THE INNER WORLD OF GOPIS

The Gopis and Cowherds of Braj: The Great Realized Souls (Brahmgyanis)

The Gopis and Cowherds (Gwalas) of Braj were not ordinary villagers, they were the embodiments of supreme spiritual realization. They did not just know Krishna from the outside as the son of Yashoda, but through the 'Brahmgyan' (Divine Knowledge) received from a Master, they saw Him directly within their own hearts as the 'Supreme Brahman'. For them, playing with Krishna or selling curd was not a worldly task, but a continuous state of deep meditation (Samadhi).

1. Inner Realization: The Same Krishna Within and Without
The devotion of the Gopis was based on 'Realization', not just 'Information'. Unlike 'Sanjaya', who only saw external events, the residents of Braj possessed the 'Divine Eye' (Third Eye). Through this, they knew that the same Krishna playing the flute before them was also vibrating within them as the 'Ajapa Japa' and the 'Divine Light'. Even when Krishna left for Mathura, the Gopis remained connected to Him because they had established Him within their heart lotus through Guru's grace.

2. Uddhav's Ego and the Realization of the Gopis
When Krishna sent the highly intellectual Uddhav to counsel the Gopis, his bookish knowledge failed before their 'Direct

Experience'. Uddhav wanted to teach them about the formless Brahman, but the Gopis proved that they were seeing that very Supreme Power within themselves. According to spiritual masters like Dongre Ji Maharaj, the Gopis taught Uddhav that true knowledge is not found in books, but is manifested as 'Light' in the heart. For the Gwalas and Gopis, Krishna was the 'In-dweller' whom they perceived in every breath.

3. The Inner Sound and the Flute's Melody

For the cowherds, Krishna's flute was not just a musical instrument, it was the external manifestation of the 'Anahad Naad' (Inner Sound) ringing within them. When Krishna played the flute, their consciousness would instantly rise above the body and reach the state of 'Turiya' (Super consciousness). Their love was not worldly, it was 'Brahmgyan' in its purest form. They had no body consciousness because they remained absorbed in the self light, just like Sage Shukadeva.

4. Vision in Every Particle: Sight Like Prahlada

Like Bhakta Prahlada, the Gwalas saw God in every particle. They shared Krishna's leftovers because they knew they were consuming the Divine Energy itself. For them, every act was a practical application of the 'Isha Upanishad' - seeing God everywhere. Their faith was not based on stories but on the 'Shaktipat' (Transmission of Power) received from a Master, which had destroyed their inner darkness and made them one with Krishna.

The life of the Gopis and Cowherds teaches us that 'believing' in God is just the beginning, but 'seeing' Him within is perfection. They were great 'Brahmgyanis' because they replaced Sanjaya's informative vision with 'Divine Vision'. This 'Divine Light' was the key that freed them from the illusion of the mortal body and gave them the experience of the eternal realm. Realization is the ultimate truth that removes the gap between the devotee and the Divine.

CHAPTER 19: LIGHT OF GARG SAMHITA

The Brajwasis in the Light of Garg Samhita: The Realization of Shrutis and Sages

According to the Garg Samhita (Goloka and Vrindavan Khanda), the Gopis and Gwalas of Braj were not ordinary beings. Sage Garga explains that when Supreme Brahman Shri Krishna decided to incarnate, the embodiments of his 'Heart Energy' and 'Divine Knowledge' also took birth. Some were 'Shruti rupa' (the Vedic hymns), some were 'Rishi rupa' (sages from the Dandaka forest) and some were 'Siddha rupa' (perfected souls). Through Guru's grace and intense penance, they had achieved 'Brahmgyan' (Divine Knowledge), allowing them to perceive Krishna as the 'Supreme Brahman' not just externally but directly within their own hearts.

1. Shruti rupa Gopis: The Manifestation of Vedic Realization
Garg Samhita states that when the Vedic hymns (Shrutis) desired to experience the blissful form of the Lord, they were born as Gopis. The essence of the Vedas is— "Tameva viditva" (Knowing Him, one crosses death). These Gopis possessed the 'Divine Eye' through which they could see that the Krishna herding cows was the same 'Imperishable Element' described in the Vedas. For them, churning curd was not a worldly chore but a continuous meditation absorbed in the rhythm of 'Ajapa Japa'.

2. Rishi rupa Gopis and Gwalas: From Penance to Tattva Darshan

The sages of Dandaka forest in the Treta Yuga, who were mesmerized by Lord Rama, were born as cowherds and Gopis in Dvapara Yuga. These sages possessed the accumulated power of years of penance and 'Brahmgyan'. Garg Samhita describes that when Krishna stepped into the forest, the consciousness of the cowherds would rise above body consciousness and merge into the light of the 'Heart Cave'. They knew that Truth itself was playing with them. For them, Krishna was not 'Information' but a living 'Realization'.

3. The Power of Goloka and the Inner Light

In Garg Samhita, the 'Raas' is not a physical act but the union of the 'Soul' with the 'Supreme Soul'. It is the state where the 'Anahad Naad' (Sound of the Flute) and the 'Divine Light' (Krishna's form) become one. The residents of Braj knew that Krishna resides in the heart of every being as that same Light discussed in the Upanishads. Sage Garga says the Gopis' bodies were at home, but their minds were absorbed in Krishna's 'Inner Radiance', which they had manifested within through Guru's power.

4. Krishna in Every Atom: Proof of 'Sarvam Khalvidam Brahma'

According to Garg Samhita, during events like the subduing of the Kaliya serpent or the lifting of Govardhan hill, the faith of the cowherds did not waver. This was because they saw Krishna as 'Omnipresent'. They knew, according to the 'Isha Upanishad' principle, that Krishna is the light within water, earth and fire. As Dongre Ji Maharaj points out, their devotion was 'post realization'. They had seen Shri Krishna as the 'Supreme Light' within themselves, making external miracles natural to them.

Garg Samhita proves that the Gopis and Cowherds of Braj were the highest 'Brahmgyanis'. They did not just hear about events like 'Sanjaya' but 'Realized' them like Sage Shukadeva. The 'Divine Vision' received through Guru's grace was what freed them from worldly illusions and made them one with the 'Krishna element'. Realization is the nectar that elevates a seeker to the status of a liberated soul.

CHAPTER 20: SAGE GARGA AND NANDA BABA

Sage Garga and Nanda Baba: The Journey from Parental Attachment to Brahman Realization

In the Garg Samhita, a very profound and scientific event occurs when Sage Garga, the royal priest of the Yadus, secretly arrives at Nanda Baba's house for the naming ceremony of Krishna and Balarama. Nanda Baba considered Krishna only as his son, which was a symbol of 'Parental Attachment' (Ignorance). Sage Garga observed that Nanda's love was 'Indirect' (Information), he was only looking at the external form. Then, Sage Garga initiated Nanda Baba into 'Brahmgyan', which transformed his 'Fatherly' emotion into the state of a 'Devotee' and a 'Witness'. This event proves that without the Guru's realization, a person cannot recognize God even while living with Him.

1. The Tattva Upadesh of Sage Garga: Truth Beyond Information

When Nanda Baba welcomed Sage Garga, the Sage made it clear that this child was no ordinary infant. According to Garg Samhita, the Sage said, "Nanda! This child is 'Narayana' Himself, He is the Primal Being praised by the Vedas." Sage Garga gave Nanda Baba the 'Indirect Knowledge' (Information) that Krishna, according to the 'Isha Upanishad' principle, is the master of every atom. However, Nanda's intellect was still in doubt because he was under the veil of Maya. Then, Sage Garga granted him the 'Divine Eye' so that he could see Krishna's true form.

2. Direct Realization (Aparoksha Sakshatkara): Seeing Krishna in the Heart

Sage Garga did not just preach to Nanda Baba, he activated the thread of 'Ajapa Japa' within him, which was connected directly to the 'Light' of the heart. As soon as the Sage's power descended into Nanda Baba, he experienced that the child playing in his courtyard was the same 'Divine Light' shining within him. In the words of Dongre Ji Maharaj, the moment the Guru placed his hand on Nanda's head, his 'Attachment' vanished and he attained 'Tattva Darshan' (Realization). Now, Krishna was not just a son to him but 'Brahman' Himself.

3. Rise of Unwavering Devotion: Faith After Vision

Garg Samhita describes that Nanda Baba's devotion changed after this initiation. He was no longer like 'Sanjaya', who only kept information about Krishna's activities, he became a 'Seer' like Shukadeva. Whenever a crisis came upon Krishna (like the killing of Putana), Nanda Baba did not get agitated because he knew the 'Almighty Brahman' was in his home. This state of fearlessness was possible only through the realization of 'Brahmgyan'. The Guru's initiation made him realize that Krishna could never be separate from him.

4. Experience of Brahman in Every Atom

By the grace of Sage Garga, Nanda Baba experienced that Krishna was not just in the house but pervaded the entire universe. According to 'Garg Samhita', Nanda Baba started hearing the vibration of Krishna's 'Anahad Naad' (Inner Sound) in every tree, vine and the soil of Gokul. This was the same 'Isha Upanishad' truth that Prahlada saw in the pillar. This realization of Nanda Baba was the real power of Braj. The 'Divine Vision' given by the Guru was the touchstone that transformed Nanda Baba's parental love into 'Divine Love'.

The dialogue between Nanda Baba and Sage Garga teaches us that even while living with God, we need a 'Guru' who can remove the veil of 'Attachment' from our eyes. Considering God as a 'son' or 'friend' is love, but seeing Him as 'Brahman' within oneself is 'Realization'. The Brahmgyan given by Sage Garga is that light which frees a person from the mortal world and merges them into the Imperishable Element.

CHAPTER 21: STORY OF MOTHER YASHODA

Mother Yashoda: The Direct Realization of the 'Universal Form' in the Courtyard of Love

In the history of spirituality, the story of Mother Yashoda is the best example of the difference between 'Information' (Paroksha) and 'Realization' (Aparoksha). Mother Yashoda considered Krishna as her son, which was the peak of her love. However, according to the 'Garg Samhita', Lord Krishna manifested the entire universe within His mouth twice to prove to His mother that the one she was cradling in her arms was the very foundation of "Sarvam Khalvidam Brahma" (All is Brahman). This event clarifies that knowing God only through 'affection' is incomplete, knowing Him through the 'Divine Vision' is perfection.

1. Vision of the Universe: Transformation of Information into Realization

When Krishna ate soil and Mother Yashoda asked Him to open His mouth, what happened was not magic but a practical manifestation of 'Brahmgyan'. In Krishna's mouth, she saw not just soil, but the entire living and moving world, the ten directions, the sun, moon, stars and even herself and Gokul. According to Garg Samhita, at that moment, Yashoda's consciousness crossed the physical and mental layers and reached the level of 'Vijnanamaya' (Intuitive wisdom). She saw directly that Krishna is the center from which the entire universe originates and into which it merges.

2. Sage Garga's Initiation and Yashoda's Awakening

Although this vision occurred through Krishna's play, it was supported by the spiritual foundation laid by Sage Garga in the house of Nanda. According to masters like Dongre Ji Maharaj, only when a Guru performs 'Shaktipat' (Transmission of Power) does the intellect become capable of beholding the 'Universal Form'. When Yashoda had this vision, she momentarily forgot her 'Attachment' (Maya) and trembled before the 'Brahman'. She realized that the 'Anahad Naad' ringing within her and the child standing before her were the same essence.

3. The Veil of Maya and the Subtlety of Guru Tattva

Immediately after the vision, the Lord covered Yashoda's realization again with His 'Vaishnavi Maya' so that her parental love could continue. This lesson teaches that even after attaining 'Brahmgyan', following the Guru's will and maintaining worldly decorum is necessary. Mother Yashoda was not like 'Sanjaya', just a neutral informer, she was a direct seer of that 'Supreme Light'. She had realized that Krishna, according to the 'Isha' truth, was shining in every pore of her being. This was why, even while nursing Krishna, she was unconsciously in the rhythm of 'Ajapa Japa'.

4. Vision in Every Particle: From Parental Love to Immortality

Garg Samhita describes that Yashoda's love was not just for a child, but for that 'Universal Form' she had seen within. Like Prahlada, she perceived the same Divine Light in the soil of Gokul and the dust of Krishna's feet. Gurudev Shri Ashutosh Maharaj Ji often explains this truth - that when the 'Divine Eye' opens, a person, like Mother Yashoda, realizes that God is not far away but extremely near, within one's own self.

The story of Mother Yashoda teaches us that having God as a 'son' is a blessing, but 'seeing' Him as 'Brahman' within oneself is the true fulfilment of life. The 'Divine Vision' received through Guru's grace is what frees us from the bonds of attachment and drowns us in the bliss of 'Darshan' (Vision). Her realization proves that God is not a subject of 'Information' but of 'Direct Experience'. When we see that 'Light' within, only then do we achieve true peace and immortality.

CHAPTER 22: VISION OF AKRURA

Akrura's Vision in the Yamuna: The 'Universal Form' and the Realization of Brahmgyan

In the journey of spirituality, the story of Akrura reveals a scientific truth - that to 'see' God, one needs the 'Divine Vision' granted by a Guru, not physical eyes. Akrura, a wise devotee, was tasked with taking Krishna to Mathura. According to the 'Garg Samhita', the event that occurred at the banks of the Yamuna was not just a miracle but a practical test of 'Brahmgyan'.

1. The Chariot and the Water: Conflict between Information and Realization

While Akrura was taking Krishna on the chariot, his faith was 'Indirect' (Information). He knew Krishna was God, but he had not seen that 'Essence' directly. While bathing in the Yamuna, he saw that the same Krishna sitting on the chariot was also present deep inside the water as Lord Narayana on the Sheshnag. This proved that Krishna is 'Omnipresent' - He is both outside and inside.

2. Manifestation of the Divine Eye: Light within the Water

According to Garg Samhita, the 'Universal Form' Akrura saw was not perceived by physical eyes. At that moment, Shri Krishna awakened Akrura's 'Divine Eye' (Third Eye). As Dongre Ji Maharaj points out, until the Guru performs

'Shaktipat', a person only sees water in water and stone in stone. Akrura saw the entire universe merging into that radiant Being. This was the same 'Adityavarnam' light described in the Upanishads.

3. Experience of Ajapa Japa and Anahad Naad

When Akrura saw that divine form, he was stunned. He felt the same 'Anahad Naad' (Inner Sound) resonating inside and outside. Gurudev Shri Ashutosh Maharaj Ji often explains that the real 'pilgrimage' is within the body. For Akrura, the Yamuna water became a medium to realize the 'Brahman Light' within. He realized that Krishna pervades every drop of water.

4. True Devotion: End of Doubt and Perfection of Vision

When Akrura came out of the water, Krishna asked with a smile, "Uncle, what did you see in the water?" Akrura replied with choked emotions, "Lord! Everything wonderful in this world is within You." This was the answer of a 'Seer', not just a scholar. Like 'Sanjaya', Akrura was no longer just an informer, he became a 'witness'. His doubt was destroyed and he realized that Krishna being on the chariot was just a play, while the whole universe resides in Him.

Akrura's story teaches us that searching for God only on the outside is not enough. Until the 'Divine Vision' is attained through Guru's grace, we will continue to see God only as a historical figure. Realizing that 'Light' within, as Akrura did, is the true goal of religion. Realization is the nectar that frees a human from worldly bonds and leads to the supreme state.

CHAPTER 23: LIBERATION OF KUBJA

The Liberation of Kubja: The End of Inner Crookedness and the Straight Path of Brahmgyan

The meeting of Shri Krishna and Kubja (Trivakra) in the streets of Mathura reveals a deep scientific truth of spirituality. Kubja, whose body had three bends (humps), is a symbol of a soul bound by 'Triple Sufferings' and the three qualities of nature. According to the 'Garg Samhita', Krishna did not just grant her physical beauty. He awakened her dormant centers of 'Brahmgyan' and led her to the state of 'Realization'.

1. The Science of Three Bends and the Sushumna Nadi
The three bends in Kubja's body represent the imbalance of the energy channels (Ida, Pingla and Sushumna) and the veil of ignorance. As long as a human has ego and vices, their consciousness remains 'crooked'. Krishna pressed her toes with His feet and lifted her chin. This act was actually a method of 'Shaktipat' (Transmission of Power), through which a Guru raises the disciple's consciousness directly to the 'Third Eye'.

2. Initiation by Touch and Opening of the Divine Eye

According to Garg Samhita, by Krishna's mere touch, Kubja's spine became straight and she transformed into a beautiful woman. But here, 'beauty' refers to inner divinity. At that moment, Krishna opened her 'Divine Eye'. As Dongre Ji Maharaj points out, Kubja experienced that the one standing before her was the same 'Divine Light' shining within her. She was no longer just an informer like 'Sanjaya', she became a 'Seer' like Sage Shukadeva.

3. Unwavering Devotion: From Information to Realization

Kubja was initially just a servant carrying sandalwood for King Kansa. She had 'Information' about Krishna, but not 'Realization'. Krishna's touch awakened the 'Ajapa Japa' and the 'Anahad Naad' within her. She became so 'Krishna-fied' that she held His garment and invited Him to her home. This invitation was a call to establish the Divine in her soul forever.

4. Vision in Every Particle and Self Realization

The Garg Samhita describes that Kubja's heart was now established in the 'Brahman state'. Like Prahlada, she no longer saw fear in Mathura, but only Krishna's Light. When consciousness flows through the 'Sushumna', only then does one truly experience 'Brahmgyan'. Kubja becoming 'straight' is a symbol of the end of her ignorance and the rise of self-realization.

The story of Kubja teaches us that we all are 'crooked' in our thoughts and actions. Until we find a Guru like Krishna, who straightens us with His power, we cannot see 'Brahman'. Believing in God is information, but 'seeing' Him within through the Guru's touch is 'Realization'. This is the ultimate truth that destroys all vices and transforms the soul into its pure, beautiful state.

CHAPTER 24: BHAKTA PRAHLADA

Bhakta Prahlada: The Seer of God in Every Atom and the Power of Brahmgyan

The story of Bhakta Prahlada in the Srimad Bhagavat Purana is a living proof of the science of 'Direct Realization' and 'Guru Initiation'. Prahlada proved that God is not limited to Vaikuntha but pervades every atom according to the principle of "Ishavasyam idam sarvam." His journey shows that spiritual light given by a Guru is what destroys the darkness of ignorance.

1. Knowledge in the Womb and Initiation after Birth: The Necessity of a Guru

The most important aspect of Prahlada's life is his refuge in a Guru. While in the womb, Devarshi Narada gave him spiritual instructions. However, just as Shukadeva was enlightened from birth but still sought King Janaka for perfection, Prahlada also needed the direct presence of a Guru after birth. The knowledge in the womb was like a 'seed' but it needed the Guru's initiation after birth to become a 'tree'. Narada connected Prahlada to the practical experience of 'Ajapa Japa' and the 'Divine Light' which kept him detached from the world.

2. Vision in Every Particle: Practical Form of Isha Upanishad

The Isha Upanishad says the entire universe is pervaded by God. Prahlada had not just heard this truth, he had 'Seen' it by the Guru's grace. When Hiranyakashipu asked, "Is your God in this pillar?" Prahlada replied with confidence, "Yes, He is in this pillar and in me and you." Only one with the 'Divine Eye' (Third Eye) can say this. For Prahlada, the pillar was not just stone, he could see the radiant God within it through the vision given by his Guru.

3. Shaktipat and the State of Fearlessness

Like Shukadeva, the grace in Prahlada's life came as 'Shaktipat' (Transmission of Power). The 'Brahmgyan' given by Narada freed him from body consciousness. This is why fire and poison could not affect him. When a Guru manifests the 'Anahad Naad' and Divine Light within, the disciple rises from being an informer like 'Sanjaya' to becoming a 'Seer'. Prahlada was so absorbed in that inner light that he did not feel any external pain.

4. True Devotion: Unwavering Faith after Realization

Prahlada's devotion was based on 'Darshan' (Vision). According to the teachings of masters like Dongre Ji Maharaj, true devotion arises only when the Guru manifests the light within by his grace. Prahlada did not need logic to 'believe' in God because he was 'seeing' Him every moment. The appearance of Lord Narasimha was the external proof of his inner vision. This story teaches that Guru's initiation is the touchstone that turns even a child into a realized soul.

Bhakta Prahlada's life shows that God is a subject of 'Vision' not logic. Brahmgyan given by the Guru is the divine sight through which one sees God in every atom. Realization is the ultimate truth that protects a seeker and leads them to immortality.

CHAPTER 25: THE SUBDUING OF KALIYA

The Subduing of Kaliya: Crushing the Hundred Vices and the Rise of Brahman Light

The subduing of the Kaliya serpent in the poisonous depths of the Yamuna is not just a tale of bravery but a manifestation of deep psychological and spiritual truths. The hundred hoods of Kaliya represent the countless desires, anger and 'Ego' within a human, which have poisoned the Yamuna of life. According to the 'Garg Samhita', Krishna's dance on those hoods is the process of 'Brahmgyan' (Divine Knowledge), where the Guru crushes the disciple's ego and connects their consciousness to the 'Supreme Light'.

1. The Hundred Hoods and the Secret of Kundalini

Kaliya's hundred hoods represent the vices surrounding the soul. As long as these vices are active, the soul suffers from the poison of 'Ignorance'. Krishna (the symbol of the Perfect Master and Brahman) struck these hoods. This spiritually signifies 'Shaktipat' (Transmission of Power). When a Guru initiates a disciple, they control the disciple's 'Mind' (the serpent) with their power. As soon as Krishna's lotus feet touched Kaliya's head, all his poison (ignorance) vanished and he became pure.

2. Anahad Naad and the Divine Dance

Garg Samhita describes that while Krishna danced on the serpent's hoods, a wondrous 'Anahad Naad' (Inner Sound) resonated throughout the universe. This dance was not a simple act but a process of piercing the 'Six Chakras' within the body. According to Dongre Ji Maharaj, when a Guru manifests 'Brahmgyan' within a disciple, the disciple experiences that 'Divine Music' and 'Light' within their own self. The bowing of Kaliya's head is proof that the 'Intellect' is now subordinate to 'Brahman'.

3. Information to Realization: The Prayer of the Nagpatnis

When Kaliya's wives prayed to Krishna, their knowledge was moving from 'Information' to 'Realization'. They realized that the boy dancing on their husband's hoods was the Lord of both water and land, according to the 'Isha Upanishad' truth. Seeing events like 'Sanjaya' was not enough for Kaliya, it was the moment of realization. Gurudev Shri Ashutosh Maharaj Ji often explains that only when Krishna (Knowledge) mounts our mind (the serpent) does the Yamuna of life become pure and we attain the 'Divine Eye'.

4. Vision in Every Particle and the Fearless State

After being subdued, Kaliya went towards the ocean without fear. This 'Fearless' state comes only after 'Realization'. Like Prahlada, Kaliya also realized that he was not a 'poisonous creature' but a part of that 'Divine Light'. Garg Samhita proves that Krishna's touch turns the impure into pure and a sinner into a realized soul. When a seeker catches the thread of 'Ajapa

Japa' within, their internal 'Kaliya' (the egoistic mind) becomes silent and becomes a servant of God.

The message of Kaliya Daman is clear - as long as the hoods of 'Ego' are high within us, we cannot experience 'Brahman'. Only the 'Brahmgyan' provided by the Guru is the power that can crush our vices and show us the direct vision of our soul. Searching for God outside is information, but making Krishna dance on the hoods of our mind (controlling it) and seeing the Light within is 'Realization'. This is the ultimate truth that turns the poison of the world into nectar.

CHAPTER 26: REALIZING BRAHMAN IN NATURE

The Govardhan Leela: Crushing Indra's Pride and Realizing Brahman in Nature

The lifting of the Govardhan Hill is the ultimate example of transforming 'Information' (Paroksha) into 'Realization' (Aparoksha). This act proves that God is not just a power living in the clouds but, according to the 'Isha' truth, He is directly present in every particle and stone of nature. By challenging Indra's ego, Shri Krishna taught the people of Braj that true worship is not just ritual based on fear, but the 'Direct Vision' of the essence that supports all creation.

1. Indra's Pride and the Illusion of Indirect Knowledge
Devraj Indra believed he was the sole master of rain. This is a symbol of 'Ego'. Krishna explained to Nanda Baba and the cowherds that they should worship Govardhan, which provides direct benefits. Krishna declared in Garg Samhita, "Govardhano girivarah sakshach chri purushottamah..." (This supreme Govardhan hill is Lord Purushottama Himself... it must be worshipped as the fulfiller of all desires.)

2. Vision of Brahman in the Mountain: The Science of the Divine Eye
When Krishna took the form of the mountain, the residents of Braj were granted the 'Divine Eye' (Third Eye). This was a

moment of 'Shaktipat' (Transmission of Power). Just as 'Sanjaya' saw the war with divine sight, the cowherds saw that the mountain was the same 'Divine Light' shining within them. As stated in Garg Samhita, "Sadyo vaikunthtam prapto govardhandharo girih..." (The Govardhan hill instantly became divine like Vaikuntha itself, shining with its own radiance).

3. Seven Days of Stability: Inner Sound and Yoga

Krishna held the hill for seven days, symbolizing the seven chakras and the completeness of life. Despite the torrential rain, the cowherds remained unafraid because they were established in the 'Anahad Naad' and inner peace. When a Guru provides the shield of 'Brahmgyan' the disciple's mind becomes perfectly stable.

4. Indra's Surrender and Realization

When Indra's ego was shattered, he realized that he only had 'Information' about Krishna, but now had the 'Realization'. In Garg Samhita, Indra prays, "Tvam brahma paramam sakshat... drashtum maya na shakyam tvamrite jnand risha vibho" (O Lord! You are the Supreme Brahman beyond nature. Without the Eye of Knowledge (Divine Vision), it is impossible to see You).

The message of Govardhan Leela is that when we awaken the 'Govardhan' (stable wisdom) within us, no worldly storm can harm us. Believing God is in a stone is information, but 'seeing' Brahman in the mountain is 'Realization'.

PART – 2: HINDI

अध्याय 1: ईश्वर दिखाई देता है

ईश्वर दर्शन योग्य है: सूचना से साक्षात्कार तक की एक दिव्य यात्रा

1. प्रत्यक्ष दर्शन की अनिवार्यता: सूचना और साक्षात्कार का अंतर मानव इतिहास में 'ईश्वर' सदैव सबसे अधिक चर्चा का विषय रहा है। भारतीय संस्कृति और उपनिषद उद्घोष करते हैं कि ईश्वर केवल विश्वास का विषय या कोई दार्शनिक विचार नहीं है; वह प्रत्यक्ष 'साक्षात्कार' (Sakshatkara) का विषय है। जैसा कि गुरुदेव सर्व श्री आशुतोष महाराज जी अक्सर कहते हैं– "यदि ईश्वर है, तो वह दिखाई भी देना चाहिए।" आध्यात्मिकता की इस वैज्ञानिक यात्रा को समझने के लिए महाभारत के 'संजय' और रामायण के 'गरुड़' के उदाहरण सर्वश्रेष्ठ हैं। इन दोनों के पास ईश्वर के विषय में 'सूचना' (Information) तो थी, लेकिन 'अनुभूति' (Realization) का अभाव था। संजय के पास दूरदर्शन की शक्ति थी जिससे वे युद्धक्षेत्र को दूर से देख सकते थे, और

गरुड़ स्वयं भगवान विष्णु के वाहन थे। फिर भी, संजय केवल बाहरी दृश्यों को देख रहे थे और गरुड़ अपने तार्किक संदेहों के जाल में फंसे थे। दोनों के पास दृष्टि तो थी, लेकिन वह 'दिव्य दृष्टि' नहीं थी जो हृदय के भीतर ईश्वर का दर्शन करा सके।

2. संदेह का अंधकार और सद्गुरु की अनिवार्यता: यह गहरा सत्य गरुड़ के संदेह की कथा से स्पष्ट होता है। जब गरुड़ ने भगवान राम को 'नागपाश' में बंधा देखा, तो उनके मन में संशय उत्पन्न हो गया, "जो स्वयं संपूर्ण ब्रह्मांड का स्वामी है, वह एक साधारण सर्प के बंधन में कैसे आ सकता है?" अज्ञान के इस अंधकार को दूर करने के लिए उन्हें काकभुशुंडि जी के पास भेजा गया। गोस्वामी तुलसीदास जी रामचरितमानस में स्पष्ट करते हैं: “गुरु बिनु भवनिधि तरइ न कोई, जौं बिरंचि संकर सम होई।।” अर्थात्, गुरु के बिना कोई भी इस संसार रूपी सागर को पार नहीं कर सकता, चाहे वह ब्रह्मा या शिव के समान शक्तिशाली ही क्यों न हो। संजय और गरुड़ दोनों ने अपने भीतर एक गहरा खालीपन महसूस किया। संजय ने अनुभव किया कि जब अर्जुन आँखें

बंद करते थे, तो उनके चेहरे पर एक दिव्य शांति चमकती थी। यही बेचैनी संजय को शुकदेव मुनि के पास और गरुड़ को काकभुशुंडि जी के पास ले गई। यहीं मानव शरीर की महत्ता समझ में आती है - यह एक दुर्लभ उपहार है जिसका उद्देश्य गुरु की खोज कर 'अंतर्मुखी' होना है।

3. भक्ति-मणि का रहस्य: हृदय का स्वयं-प्रकाशित नूर

काकभुशुंडि जी और शुकदेव मुनि ने उन्हें 'भक्ति-मणि' के गुप्त रहस्य से परिचित कराया। वास्तविक भक्ति केवल बाहरी कर्मकांड नहीं है; यह वह प्रकाश है जो हृदय के भीतर जलता है। तुलसीदास जी इसका वर्णन इस प्रकार करते हैं: "परम प्रकास रूप दिन राती, नहिं कछु चहिए दिआ घृत बाती।" इसका अर्थ है कि इस आंतरिक प्रकाश को किसी तेल, घी या बत्ती की आवश्यकता नहीं है, यह आत्मा का स्वयं-चमकता हुआ स्वरूप है। जैसे बादल सूर्य को ढक लेते हैं, वैसे ही हमारे विचार और अज्ञान इस प्रकाश को छिपा देते हैं। जब तक एक पूर्ण सद्गुरु 'दिव्य चक्षु' (तीसरा नेत्र) नहीं

खोलते, मनुष्य सूचनाओं की दुनिया में ही भटकता रहता है। वास्तविक भक्ति तभी शुरू होती है जब आंतरिक अंधकार का पूर्णतः विनाश हो जाता है।

4. ब्रह्मज्ञान के बाद ही सच्ची भक्ति का प्रारंभ: यहाँ एक अनिवार्य सत्य को समझना होगा: वास्तविक भक्ति (Bhakti) का प्रारंभ 'ब्रह्मज्ञान' (Divine Knowledge) के माध्यम से ईश्वर के शाश्वत अनुभव के बाद ही होता है। अक्सर लोग सोचते हैं कि भक्ति करने से ईश्वर मिलेगा। लेकिन शास्त्र कहते हैं–आप उससे प्रेम (भक्ति) कैसे कर सकते हैं जिसे आपने कभी देखा या जिससे कभी मिले ही नहीं? काकभुशुंडि जी ने गरुड़ को समझाया कि जब तक हृदय के भीतर 'भक्ति-मणि' का प्रकाश प्रकट नहीं होता, मनुष्य मानसिक रोगों और संदेहों से त्रस्त रहता है।

जब व्यक्ति गुरु की शक्ति के माध्यम से अपने भीतर ईश्वर को देख लेता है, तो उसका 'विश्वास' 'निश्चितता' में बदल जाता है। यह वह क्षण है जब व्यक्ति पहले 'जानता' है और फिर 'मानता' है। यही सच्ची और निस्वार्थ भक्ति का प्रारंभिक बिंद है।

5. आध्यात्मिक विस्फोट: आत्म-दर्शन से संदेहों की मुक्ति 'ब्रह्मज्ञान' की विधि वह वैज्ञानिक मार्ग है जो एक जिज्ञासु को सच्चे भक्त में बदल देती है। जब शुकदेव मुनि ने संजय को और काकभुशुंडि जी ने गरुड़ को दीक्षित किया, तो उनके भीतर एक आध्यात्मिक विस्फोट हुआ। वह 'विराट स्वरूप' और हजारों सूर्यों का प्रकाश, जिसका वे पहले केवल शब्दों में वर्णन करते थे, अब उनके भीतर स्पष्ट रूप से प्रकट हो गया। जब गरुड़ ने अपने भीतर राम के वास्तविक स्वरूप को देखा, तो उनके सभी संदेह और मानसिक पीड़ाएं सदा के लिए शांत हो गईं। इस अनुभव ने 'विष को अमृत' में बदल दिया। गुरु द्वारा दी गई यह आंतरिक दृष्टि (Insight) किसी भी आधुनिक तकनीक या बाहरी दृष्टि से कहीं अधिक महान है।

निष्कर्षतः "ईश्वर दर्शन योग्य है" केवल एक नारा नहीं, बल्कि एक जीवंत सत्य है। आज का आधुनिक मानव संजय की भाँति इंटरनेट और पुस्तकों की सूचनाओं से परिपूर्ण है, किन्तु आंतरिक शांति से वंचित है, क्योंकि वह केवल 'बाहर' देख रहा है। धर्म का वास्तविक अर्थ है 'जानना', और

जानना तभी पूर्ण होता है जब हम 'देखते' हैं। एक पूर्ण सद्गुरु की कृपा से, व्यक्ति अपनी भौतिक आँखें बंद करके उस दिव्य प्रकाश का अनुभव कर सकता है। जब ईश्वर केवल एक विचार न रहकर हमारे भीतर 'दृश्यमान सत्य' (Visible Truth) बन जाता है, तभी जीवन सफल होता है और सच्ची भक्ति का जन्म होता है। गुरुदेव सर्व श्री आशुतोष महाराज जी इसी दिव्य जागृति का आह्वान करते हैं।

अध्याय 2: ब्रह्मज्ञान

ब्रह्मज्ञान: अज्ञान की भस्म से आत्म-साक्षात्कार के दिव्य जागरण तक

1. अज्ञान की भस्म से आत्म-साक्षात्कार की ओर: सती का संदेह और मानसिक द्वंद्व आध्यात्मिक यात्रा का अर्थ है 'संदेह' से 'सत्य' की ओर गमन। गुरुदेव सर्व श्री आशुतोष महाराज जी अक्सर समझाते हैं कि रामचरितमानस में माता सती की कथा केवल एक पौराणिक प्रसंग नहीं, बल्कि मानवीय अहंकार और दिव्य वास्तविकता के बीच होने वाले द्वंद्व का प्रतिनिधित्व करती है। जब सती ने भगवान राम को वन में माता सीता के वियोग में रोते देखा, तो उनके तर्कप्रधान मस्तिष्क ने उन पर संदेह किया। उन्होंने सोचा, "जो ईश्वर दुख में विलाप कर रहा है, वह सर्वशक्तिमान कैसे हो सकता है?" गुरुदेव सर्व श्री आशुतोष महाराज जी कहते हैं कि भगवान शिव द्वारा बार-बार समझाने के बावजूद, सती ने अपनी बुद्धि का उपयोग कर राम की परीक्षा लेने का निर्णय लिया।

उन्होंने सीता का वेश धारण किया, परंतु अंतर्यामी प्रभु राम ने उन्हें तुरंत पहचान लिया और उन्हें 'माता' कहकर संबोधित करते हुए पूछा, "भगवान शिव कहाँ हैं?" यह कथा सिद्ध करती है कि ईश्वर को बाहरी आँखों या चालाकी से नहीं पहचाना जा सकता। जब सती ने अपने सीमित मन से उन्हें समझना चाहा, तो वे असफल रहीं। महाराज जी बल देते हैं कि जब तक अहंकार का पर्दा नहीं हटता, सत्य का दर्शन असंभव है। जैसा कि मानस में आता है: "सतिहि दीख जहाँ जहाँ चितवही, तहँ तहँ रामु सहित श्री रही" (सती जहाँ भी देखतीं, उन्हें हर ओर प्रभु राम और माँ लक्ष्मी के दर्शन होने लगे)।

2. बुद्धि का विसर्जन और सती का आत्मदाह: देह-बुद्धि की समाप्ति सती द्वारा सीता का रूप धारण करना एक गंभीर आध्यात्मिक त्रुटि थी, क्योंकि उन्होंने जगज्जननी का स्थान लेने का प्रयास किया। गुरुदेव सर्व श्री आशुतोष महाराज जी समझाते हैं कि इस कारण भगवान शिव ने उनके साथ सांसारिक संबंध त्यागने का संकल्प किया: "सती कीन्ह सीता कर बेषा, सिव उर भयउ बिषाद बिसेषा।" इसके पश्चात, जब

सती अपने पिता दक्ष के यज्ञ में गईं और वहां शिव का अपमान देखा, तो वे उसे सहन नहीं कर सकीं और उन्होंने योगाग्नि में अपना शरीर त्याग दिया। महाराज जी के अनुसार, यह "जलना" उस 'पुरानी बुद्धि' का अंत था जो ईश्वर को केवल एक हाड़-मांस के शरीर के रूप में देखती थी। श्रीमद्भगवद्गीता (2.22) में भगवान कहते हैं: वासांसि जीर्णानि यथा विहाय नवानि गृह्णाति नरोऽपराणि। अर्थात् जैसे मनुष्य पुराने वस्त्र त्यागकर नए धारण करता है, वैसे ही आत्मा शरीर बदलती है। सती का यह बलिदान उनकी अगली जन्म की यात्रा का आधार बना, जहाँ वे 'परीक्षा' लेने वाली सती से 'अनुभूति' करने वाली पार्वती की ओर अग्रसर हुईं।

3. पार्वती का तप और गुरुदेव का सानिध्य: ब्रह्मज्ञान की प्राप्ति हिमालय की पुत्री पार्वती के रूप में जन्म लेकर उन्होंने कठोर तपस्या की। गुरुदेव सर्व श्री आशुतोष महाराज जी स्पष्ट करते हैं कि इस बार वे गुरु की 'परीक्षा' लेने नहीं, बल्कि उनसे 'दीक्षित' होने आई थीं। भगवान शिव, जो साक्षात 'जगतगुरु' हैं, ने उन्हें 'ब्रह्मज्ञान' प्रदान किया। गुरु गीता में

कहा गया है: गुरुर्ब्रह्मा गुरुर्विष्णु गुरुर्देवो महेश्वरः। गुरुः साक्षात् परब्रह्म तस्मै श्रीगुरवे नमः॥ शिव ने पार्वती का 'दिव्य चक्षु' (तीसरा नेत्र) खोला और उन्हें उनके भीतर ही उसी प्रकाश का दर्शन कराया जिसे वे पिछले जन्म में बाहर खोज रही थीं। शिव ने समझाया कि राम केवल दशरथ पुत्र नहीं, बल्कि प्रत्येक घट में निवास करने वाला 'शाश्वत प्रकाश' (Eternal Light) हैं। गुरु गीता इस सत्य की पुष्टि करती है: "अज्ञान-तिमिरान्धस्य ज्ञानाञ्जन-शलाकया" (अज्ञान के अंधकार में अंधे हुए व्यक्ति की आँखों को गुरु ज्ञान रूपी शलाका से खोल देते हैं)। गुरुदेव सर्व श्री आशुतोष महाराज जी कहते हैं कि सच्चा ज्ञान केवल पुस्तकों में नहीं, बल्कि गुरु द्वारा प्रदत्त आंतरिक प्रकाश में है।

4. ब्रह्मज्ञान का विज्ञान: प्रत्यक्ष अनुभूति बनाम सूचना यह समझना अत्यंत आवश्यक है कि 'ब्रह्मज्ञान' केवल सूचना का संग्रह नहीं है, बल्कि यह आत्मा का विज्ञान है। गुरुदेत सर्त श्री आशुतोष महाराज जी के अनुसार, जब पार्वती भगवान शिव द्वारा दीक्षित हुईं, तब उन्हें अहसास हुआ कि जिस सत्य की खोज में वे भटक रही थीं, वह वास्तव में उनके

'भ्रूमध्य' (आज्ञा चक्र) के पीछे स्थित था। यही वह क्षण था जब उनकी वास्तविक 'भक्ति' का प्रारंभ हुआ। उपनिषद कहते हैं: "तद्विज्ञानार्थं स गुरुमेवाभिगच्छेत्" (सत्य को जानने के लिए गुरु की शरण में जाना अनिवार्य है)। सती इसलिए असफल रहीं क्योंकि उनके पास केवल 'सूचना' थी, जबकि पार्वती इसलिए सफल हुईं क्योंकि उनके पास गुरु द्वारा दी गई 'अनुभूति' थी। गुरुदेव सर्व श्री आशुतोष महाराज जी समझाते हैं कि दिव्य चक्षु के बिना ईश्वर के वास्तविक स्वरूप को देखना असंभव है, ठीक वैसे ही जैसे अर्जुन तब तक विराट रूप नहीं देख सके जब तक श्रीकृष्ण ने उन्हें दिव्य दृष्टि नहीं दी।

निष्कर्षतः सती से पार्वती तक की यात्रा प्रत्येक साधक की आत्मिक यात्रा है। गुरुदेव सर्व श्री आशुतोष महाराज जी के शब्दों में, जब तक मनुष्य अपने मन के अहंकार से ईश्वर की 'परीक्षा' लेता है, वह 'भस्म' (पतन) की ओर जाता है। किंतु जब वह एक पूर्ण सद्गुरु (जैसे शिव) के चरणों में पूर्ण समर्पण कर अपने 'दिव्य चक्षु' को जाग्रत करता है, तब उसे सर्वशक्तिमान के वास्तविक स्वरूप का दर्शन होता है। गुरु

की कृपा से प्राप्त 'ब्रह्मज्ञान' वह प्रकाश है जो संदेह के सारे अंधकार को मिटा देता है। जैसा कि गुरु गीता कहती है: "न गुरोरधिकं तत्त्वं" (गुरु से बढ़कर कोई सत्य नहीं है)। जब भीतर प्रकाश प्रकट होता है, तभी मनुष्य को यह आभास होता है कि ईश्वर कहीं दूर नहीं, बल्कि शाश्वत रूप से हमारे भीतर ही विराजमान है। गुरुदेव सर्व श्री आशुतोष महाराज जी इसी प्रत्यक्ष दर्शन पर बल देते हैं ताकि प्रत्येक आत्मा अपने मूल स्वरूप को पहचान सके।

अध्याय 3: मृत्यु से अमरत्व

मृत्यु से अमरत्व की ओर: नचिकेता की जिज्ञासा और ब्रह्मज्ञान की अनुभूति

उपनिषदों का सार "अन्धकार से प्रकाश की ओर" (तमसो मा ज्योतिर्गमय) की यात्रा है। कठोपनिषद में, बालक नचिकेता और यमराज के बीच का संवाद इस यात्रा का एक वैज्ञानिक और आध्यात्मिक मानचित्र प्रदान करता है। जब नचिकेता ने अपने पिता को बूढ़ी और अनुपयोगी गायों का दान करते देखा, तो उनका हृदय पूर्ण सत्य को जानने की इच्छा से भर गया। वे यमराज (मृत्यु के राजा) के द्वार पर पहुँचे और बिना अन्न-जल के तीन दिनों तक प्रतीक्षा की। यह धैर्य इस बात का प्रतीक है कि ब्रह्मज्ञान (दिव्य ज्ञान) का मार्ग केवल उसी साधक के लिए खुलता है जिसमें सच्चा दृढ़ संकल्प और सांसारिक इच्छाओं से वैराग्य हो। नचिकेता की परीक्षा लेने के लिए, यमराज ने उन्हें सोना, लंबी आयु और संसार के सभी सुखों का प्रलोभन दिया। हालाँकि, नचिकेता ने उन्हें यह

कहते हुए अस्वीकार कर दिया: "श्वोभावा मर्त्यस्य यदन्तकैतत्" (हे मृत्यु के देवता, ये सभी सुख क्षणिक हैं और कल समाप्त हो जाएंगे)।

नचिकेता का वैराग्य सिद्ध करता है कि आध्यात्मिक संतुष्टि केवल सूचना या भौतिक वस्तुओं से प्राप्त नहीं की जा सकती। नचिकेता की पात्रता देखकर, यमराज ने उन्हें 'ब्रह्म-विद्या' प्रदान की—वह ज्ञान जिसके बाद कुछ भी जानना शेष नहीं रहता। उन्होंने समझाया कि आत्मा न कभी जन्म लेती है और न कभी मरती है: "न जायते म्रियते वा विपश्चित्।" लेकिन इसे जानना केवल शब्दों या दर्शन का विषय नहीं है। यमराज ने नचिकेता को 'दिव्य चक्षु' (तीसरे नेत्र) के रहस्य से परिचित कराया। उन्होंने समझाया कि सर्वशक्तिमान ईश्वर हृदय के भीतर 'अंगुष्ठ मात्र' (अंगूठे के आकार के) प्रकाश के रूप में निवास करता है। जिस प्रकार सती को शिव की और पार्वती को गुरु की आवश्यकता थी, उसी प्रकार नचिकेता को इस प्रकाश को देखने के लिए यमराज के रूप में एक 'पूर्ण गुरु' (सद्गुरु) की आवश्यकता थी। इस कथा का एक प्रमुख वैज्ञानिक हिस्सा 'श्रेय' (परम कल्याण

का मार्ग) और 'प्रेय' (क्षणिक सुख का मार्ग) के बीच का अंतर है। यमराज कहते हैं कि संसार दो मार्ग प्रदान करता है: एक वह जो इंद्रियों को अच्छा लगता है लेकिन बंधन की ओर ले जाता है, और दूसरा वह जो आत्मा की मुक्ति की ओर ले जाता है।

एक सच्चा गुरु वही है जो साधक का ध्यान बाहरी दुनिया से हटाकर आंतरिक प्रकाश की ओर मोड़ दे। यहाँ गुरु गीता का सिद्धांत पूर्णतः लागू होता है: गुरु के बिना ज्ञान असंभव है। जब यमराज ने नचिकेता को ब्रह्मज्ञान की शाश्वत विधि में दीक्षित किया, तो उनके भीतर वह 'दिव्य प्रकाश' प्रकट हुआ जो सूर्य, चंद्रमा या अग्नि से परे है। उपनिषद कहता है: "तमेव भान्तमनुभाति सर्वं..." (जब वह चमकता है, तो सब कुछ चमकता है; उसके प्रकाश से ही संपूर्ण ब्रह्मांड प्रकाशित होता है)। यह स्पष्ट करना महत्वपूर्ण है कि नचिकेता को जो ज्ञान प्राप्त हुआ वह केवल एक विचार नहीं, बल्कि एक 'स्थायी अनुभूति' (Permanent Realization) थी। दिव्य दृष्टि प्राप्त करने के बाद ही नचिकेता ने अनुभव किया कि जो ईश्वर ब्रह्मांड में व्याप्त है, वही प्रकाश की एक लौ के

रूप में उनके भीतर भी उपस्थित है। उनकी सच्ची भक्ति और शांति इस प्रत्यक्ष 'साक्षात्कार' के बाद ही शुरू हुई। इस प्रत्यक्ष अनुभव के बिना मृत्यु का भय समाप्त नहीं हो सकता।

यमराज ने यह स्पष्ट कर दिया कि आध्यात्मिकता कोई जादू नहीं, बल्कि एक सूक्ष्म विज्ञान है, जिसे अक्सर 'असिधारा व्रत' (स्तुरे की धार पर चलने) के समान बताया गया है, जहाँ गुरु का मार्गदर्शन अनिवार्य है। निष्कर्षतः, नचिकेता की कथा हमें सिखाती है कि हम चाहे कितने भी विद्वान क्यों न बन जाएँ, मृत्यु का रहस्य और ईश्वर का वास्तविक स्वरूप तब तक अनसुलझा रहता है जब तक हम अपने 'दिव्य चक्षु' को जाग्रत करने के लिए एक पूर्ण गुरु की खोज नहीं करते। नचिकेता ने ब्रह्मज्ञान के माध्यम से अमरत्व प्राप्त किया। आज भी, यदि कोई साधक सूचना की दुनिया से अनुभूति की दुनिया में जाना चाहता है, तो उसे एक ऐसे गुरु को खोजना होगा जो उसे प्रकाश दिखा सके। जब हम अपने भीतर दिव्य प्रकाश को देखते हैं, तभी हमें

आभास होता है कि हम शरीर नहीं, बल्कि अजर-अमर आत्मा हैं। यही मानव जीवन का अंतिम लक्ष्य है।

अध्याय 4: “तत्वमसि”

“तत्वमसि”: सूचना के अहंकार से अनुभूति के सत्य तक की यात्रा

अध्यात्म का वास्तविक अर्थ केवल वेदों और शास्त्रों को कंठस्थ करना नहीं है, बल्कि उस 'सत्य' को स्वयं के भीतर देखना है। छान्दोग्य उपनिषद् में ऋषि आरुणि और उनके पुत्र श्वेतकेतु का संवाद इस तथ्य का जीवंत प्रमाण है। श्वेतकेतु ने बारह वर्षों तक गुरुकुल में रहकर समस्त वेदों और शास्त्रों का अध्ययन किया, जिससे उनके भीतर विद्वत्ता का अहंकार आ गया। जब वे घर लौटे, तो पिता आरुणि ने देखा कि श्वेतकेतु के पास 'सूचना' तो बहुत है, पर 'शांति' और 'अनुभूति' का अभाव है। पिता ने एक क्रांतिकारी प्रश्न पूछा– "श्वेतकेतु! क्या तुमने उस 'तत्व' को जान लिया है जिसे जानने के बाद अनसुना भी सुना हुआ हो जाता है और अज्ञात भी ज्ञात हो जाता है?" श्वेतकेतु निरुत्तर हो गए। यह प्रसंग

सिद्ध करता है कि बाहरी शिक्षा केवल 'सूचना' है, जबकि 'ब्रह्मज्ञान' आत्मा का साक्षात्कार है।

श्वेतकेतु की जिज्ञासा जागृत होने पर ऋषि आरुणि ने उन्हें विभिन्न वैज्ञानिक उदाहरणों से समझाया कि जैसे एक मिट्टी के ढेले को जानने से मिट्टी से बनी सभी वस्तुओं का ज्ञान हो जाता है, वैसे ही उस एक परमात्मा को जानने से संपूर्ण सृष्टि का रहस्य खुल जाता है। पिता ने श्वेतकेतु को आदेश दिया कि वह पानी में नमक डालकर अगले दिन आए। अगले दिन जब श्वेतकेतु आए, तो पिता ने कहा– "उस नमक को निकालो।" श्वेतकेतु उसे देख नहीं सके क्योंकि वह घुल चुका था। पिता ने समझाया कि जैसे नमक पानी के कण-कण में व्याप्त है पर दिखाई नहीं देता, वैसे ही परमात्मा इस शरीर और ब्रह्मांड के कण-कण में है, पर इन स्थूल आँखों से ओझल है। इसे देखने के लिए 'दिव्य चक्षु' की आवश्यकता होती है।

गुरु रूप में पिता आरुणि ने श्वेतकेतु को नौ बार "स य एषोऽणिमैतदात्म्यमिदं सर्वं तत्सत्यं स आत्मा तत्त्वमसि

श्वेतकेतो" (वह जो सूक्ष्म तत्व है, वही सबका मूल है, वही सत्य है, वही आत्मा है और हे श्वेतकेतु! वह तुम ही हो) का उपदेश दिया। 'तत्वमसि' का यह उपदेश केवल एक वाक्य नहीं था, बल्कि श्वेतकेतु को उनके भीतर की उस शाश्वत ज्योति से जोड़ने की प्रक्रिया थी। जब ऋषि आरुणि ने श्वेतकेतु को ब्रह्मज्ञान में दीक्षित किया, तब श्वेतकेतु ने अपनी आँखों को बंद करके उस सूक्ष्म से भी सूक्ष्म तत्व का साक्षात्कार किया। गुरु गीता के अनुसार, गुरु ही अज्ञान के अंजन को हटाकर ज्ञान की ज्योति जलाते हैं: "अज्ञानतिमिरान्धस्य ज्ञानाञ्जनशलाकया।"

इस कथा का सबसे महत्वपूर्ण पक्ष यह है कि ब्रह्मज्ञान के बाद ही 'असल भक्ति' और 'समर्पण' का जन्म होता है। जब तक श्वेतकेतु केवल ग्रंथों के ज्ञाता थे, वे अहंकारी थे। किंतु जब गुरु कृपा से उन्हें 'दिव्य दृष्टि' मिली और उन्होंने स्वयं को उस परम प्रकाश के अंश के रूप में देखा, तब उनका अहंकार गल गया। उपनिषद कहता है कि ब्रह्म का ज्ञान होने पर व्यक्ति स्वयं ब्रह्ममय हो जाता है: “ब्रह्मविद् ब्रह्मैव भवति।” यह साक्षात्कार ही वह क्षण है जहाँ से जीव की

आध्यात्मिक यात्रा पूर्णता की ओर बढ़ती है। बिना प्रत्यक्ष दर्शन के 'तत्त्वमसि' (वह तुम हो) कहना केवल एक सूचना है, परंतु दर्शन के बाद यह एक 'अनुभूति' बन जाती है।

निष्कर्षतः श्वेतकेतु की कथा आज के आधुनिक समाज के लिए एक महान संदेश है। हम डिग्रियों और सूचनाओं के भार तले दबे हुए 'संजय' तो बन गए हैं, लेकिन हमारे भीतर 'श्वेतकेतु' जैसी व्याकुलता की कमी है। जब तक हम एक पूर्ण सतगुरु की शरण में जाकर अपने भीतर उस 'नमक की तरह व्याप्त' परमात्मा का साक्षात दर्शन नहीं करते, तब तक हमारा ज्ञान अधूरा है। 'तत्त्वमसि' का वास्तविक अर्थ तभी सिद्ध होता है जब गुरु की कृपा से हमारे 'दिव्य चक्षु' खुलते हैं और हम अपनी आत्मा को उस परमात्मा में विलीन होते हुए देखते हैं। यही साक्षात्कार मानव जीवन का परम लक्ष्य है।

अध्याय 5: सनातन सत्य का अन्वेषण

सनातन सत्य का अन्वेषण: अज्ञान के तिमिर से ब्रह्म-साक्षात्कार का वैज्ञानिक मार्ग

मानव चेतना की विकास यात्रा सदैव 'बाहर' से 'भीतर' की ओर रही है। भारतीय उपनिषद और श्रीरामचरितमानस जैसे ग्रंथ इस बात के जीवंत प्रमाण हैं कि परमात्मा केवल चर्चा या आस्था का विषय नहीं, बल्कि एक 'अनुभव' (Experience) है। अध्यात्म का यह विज्ञान स्पष्ट करता है कि जब तक मनुष्य अपनी स्थूल आँखों से संसार को देखता है, वह मोह और भ्रम में रहता है। किंतु जब एक पूर्ण सतगुरु की कृपा से उसके 'दिव्य चक्षु' (Third Eye) का उद्घाटन होता है, तब वह 'सत्य' का साक्षात दर्शन करता है। माता सती का पार्वती बनना, नचिकेता का यमराज से संवाद और श्वेतकेतु की ऋषि आरुणि से शिक्षा–ये तीनों कथाएँ अलग-अलग कालखंडों की होते हुए भी एक ही सत्य को उद्घाटित

करती हैं: "ईश्वर दिखाई देता है, और उसे देखने के लिए गुरु द्वारा प्रदत्त दिव्य दृष्टि अनिवार्य है।"

1. सती से पार्वती: तर्क के भस्म से भक्ति के उदय तक

माता सती का प्रसंग मानवीय बुद्धि के अहंकार का चरम है। जब उन्होंने प्रभु राम को एक साधारण मनुष्य की भांति सीता के लिए रोते देखा, तो उनकी 'सूचना आधारित बुद्धि' ने संदेह किया। शिव के समझाने पर भी उन्होंने परीक्षा ली और सीता का रूप धारण किया। यह मर्यादा का उल्लंघन था, जिसके कारण शिव ने उनसे नाता तोड़ लिया। सती का अपने पिता के यज्ञ में योगाग्नि द्वारा स्वयं को भस्म कर देना वास्तव में उस 'तर्क प्रधान बुद्धि' का अंत था। अगले जन्म में पार्वती के रूप में उन्होंने 'परीक्षा' के स्थान पर 'तप' और 'दीक्षा' को चुना। भगवान शिव ने जब पार्वती को गुरु रूप में 'ब्रह्मज्ञान' प्रदान किया और उनके भीतर की ज्योति जाग्रत की, तब उन्हें बोध हुआ कि राम कोई देह नहीं, बल्कि अजन्मा ब्रह्म हैं। गुरु गीता का श्लोक इसे पुष्ट करता है: "अज्ञानतिमिरान्धस्य ज्ञानाञ्जनशलाकया। चक्षुरुन्मीलितं येन

तस्मै श्रीगुरवे नमः॥" अर्थात् गुरु ने अपनी ज्ञान रूपी सलाई से पार्वती की अज्ञान की बंद आँखें खोल दीं।

2. नचिकेता का वैराग्य: मृत्यु के द्वार पर अमरत्व की खोज

कठोपनिषद् की कथा नचिकेता के माध्यम से यह समझाती है कि संसार के क्षणभंगुर सुख (प्रेय मार्ग) कभी आत्मिक शांति नहीं दे सकते। यमराज ने नचिकेता को समस्त स्वर्ग के सुखों का प्रलोभन दिया, पर नचिकेता अपनी जिज्ञासा पर अडिग रहे– "मुझे वह ज्ञान चाहिए जिससे मृत्यु का भय मिट जाए।" यमराज, जो यहाँ एक पूर्ण गुरु की भूमिका में हैं, उन्होंने नचिकेता को हृदय गुहा में स्थित उस 'अंगुष्ठमात्र' ज्योति का साक्षात कराया। यमराज ने स्पष्ट किया कि परमात्मा न वाणी से, न बुद्धि से और न बहुत सुनने से प्राप्त होता है; वह तो केवल गुरु द्वारा प्रदान की गई 'दिव्य अनुभूति' से प्राप्त होता है। नचिकेता को प्राप्त हुआ यह 'ब्रह्मज्ञान' कोई दार्शनिक विचार नहीं था, बल्कि प्रकाश का वह साक्षात्कार था जिसके बाद मृत्यु भी एक उत्सव बन गई। यहाँ "तमेव भान्तमनुभाति सर्वं" का सिद्धांत चरितार्थ हुआ, जहाँ साधक अपने भीतर ब्रह्मांड के प्रकाश को देखता है।

3. श्वेतकेतु और 'तत्वमसि': सूचना के बोझ से मुक्ति

छान्दोग्य उपनिषद् में श्वेतकेतु की कथा आज के आधुनिक मनुष्य का दर्पण है। बारह वर्षों तक शास्त्रों के अध्ययन के बाद श्वेतकेतु ज्ञान के अहंकार से भर गए थे। उनके पिता और गुरु ऋषि आरुणि ने पहचान लिया कि यह ज्ञान केवल 'सूचना' (Information) है, 'शांति' (Peace) नहीं। आरुणि ने पानी और नमक के वैज्ञानिक उदाहरण से समझाया कि जैसे नमक पानी में व्याप्त होकर भी दिखता नहीं, वैसे ही ब्रह्म इस शरीर में है पर इन आँखों से ओझल है। आरुणि ने जब श्वेतकेतु को नौ बार "तत्वमसि" (वह तुम हो) का उपदेश दिया, तो वह केवल शब्द नहीं थे, बल्कि 'शक्तिपात' की वह प्रक्रिया थी जिसने श्वेतकेतु के अंतर्जगत को प्रकाशित कर दिया। ब्रह्मज्ञान की इस शाश्वत अनुभूति के बाद ही श्वेतकेतु का अहंकार गला और उनकी 'असल भक्ति' का आरम्भ हुआ।

4. गुरु की अनिवार्यता और ब्रह्मज्ञान का विज्ञान: इन तीनों प्रसंगों में एक बात समान है–बिना गुरु के किसी को भी सत्य का दर्शन नहीं हुआ। रामचरितमानस कहती है: "गुरु बिनु भव निधि तरइ न कोई। जौं बिरंचि संकर सम होई॥" गुरु वह

वैज्ञानिक है जो मनुष्य के 'भ्रूमध्य' (तीसरे नेत्र) पर स्थित उस केंद्र को सक्रिय करता है जहाँ आत्मा का साक्षात्कार होता है। यह प्रक्रिया कोई जादू नहीं, बल्कि आत्मा का विज्ञान है। गुरु गीता स्पष्ट करती है कि गुरु ही साक्षात महेश्वर है जो अज्ञान के अंधकार को मिटाकर भीतर का सूर्य प्रकट करता है। 'ब्रह्मज्ञान' की दीक्षा के बाद ही जीव यह जान पाता है कि वह शरीर नहीं, बल्कि साक्षात ब्रह्म का अंश है। जब तक यह प्रत्यक्ष अनुभव नहीं होता, तब तक भक्ति केवल एक मानसिक कल्पना बनी रहती है।

निष्कर्ष: साक्षात्कार ही जीवन की पूर्णता है| सती, नचिकेता और श्वेतकेतु की यात्राएँ हमें यह सिखाती हैं कि धर्म का अर्थ केवल पूजा-पाठ या ग्रंथों को पढ़ना नहीं, बल्कि 'स्वयं को जानना' है। आज के युग में भी, गुरुदेव श्री आशुतोष महाराज जी इसी सनातन 'ब्रह्मज्ञान' पद्धति के माध्यम से मनुष्य को भीतर मुड़ने का मार्ग दिखा रहे हैं। जब ईश्वर 'भीतर' दिखाई देता है, तभी संदेह मिटते हैं, मृत्यु का भय समाप्त होता है और अहंकार का नाश होता है। यह 'दिव्य दृष्टि' ही वह सेतु है जो हमें सूचना के संसार से निकालकर

साक्षात्कार के जगत में ले जाती है। जिस दिन मनुष्य अपने भीतर उस "हजार सूर्यों के प्रकाश" को देख लेता है, उसी दिन उसकी आध्यात्मिक यात्रा सफल होती है और वह जीवन की सार्थकता को प्राप्त करता है।

अध्याय 6: द्वैत के भ्रम से अद्वैत

दो पक्षी और एक वृक्ष: द्वैत के भ्रम से अद्वैत के साक्षात्कार तक की यात्रा

अध्यात्म का सबसे बड़ा रहस्य यह समझना है कि हम कौन हैं और हमारा उस परम सत्ता के साथ क्या संबंध है। मुण्डकोपनिषद् में ऋषि अंगिरा अपने शिष्य शौनक को एक अत्यंत सुंदर और वैज्ञानिक दृष्टांत के माध्यम से 'ब्रह्मज्ञान' का बोध कराते हैं। वे कहते हैं कि एक ही शरीर रूपी वृक्ष पर दो सुंदर पंखों वाले पक्षी (जीवात्मा और परमात्मा) सदा साथ रहते हैं– "द्वा सुपर्णा सयुजा सखाया समानं वृक्षं परिषस्वजाते"। इनमें से एक पक्षी (जीव) वृक्ष के फलों (कर्मफल) को स्वाद ले-लेकर खाता है, जबकि दूसरा पक्षी (ईश्वर) बिना कुछ खाए केवल दृष्टा भाव से देख रहा है। यह प्रसंग सिद्ध करता है कि हम परमात्मा के अत्यंत निकट होकर भी अज्ञान के कारण उनसे अलग अनुभव करते हैं।

इस कथा का वैज्ञानिक विश्लेषण यह है कि जब तक जीव (पक्षी) संसार के सुख-दुख रूपी फल खाने में व्यस्त रहता है, वह दुखी और अशांत रहता है। वह 'संजय' की तरह केवल बाहरी दृश्यों में उलझा रहता है। मुण्डकोपनिषद् के अनुसार, जीव का दुख तब समाप्त होता है जब वह अपनी दृष्टि को फल से हटाकर अपने 'सखा' यानी उस दूसरे साक्षी पक्षी (परमात्मा) की ओर फेरता है– "तयोरन्यः पिप्पलं स्वाद्वत्त्यनश्नन्नन्यो अभिचाकशीति"। लेकिन यह दृष्टि तभी मुड़ती है जब जीव को एक 'ब्रह्मनिष्ठ' गुरु प्राप्त होता है, जो उसे यह समझा सके कि वह कर्मों का दास नहीं, बल्कि साक्षात ब्रह्म का अंश है।

गुरु की भूमिका यहाँ निर्णायक है। उपनिषद कहता है कि उस अक्षर ब्रह्म को जानने के लिए हाथ में समिधा लेकर (विनम्रता के साथ) गुरु की शरण में जाना अनिवार्य है– "तद्विज्ञानार्थं स गुरुमेवाभिगच्छेत्"। जैसे सती को पार्वती बनकर शिव की शरण लेनी पड़ी और नचिकेता को यमराज की, वैसे ही शौनक ने ऋषि अंगिरा से दीक्षा ली। गुरु ने जब 'ब्रह्मज्ञान' की पद्धति से शौनक के 'दिव्य चक्षु' को जाग्रत

किया, तब उन्हें बोध हुआ कि वह दूसरा 'साक्षी पक्षी' कोई और नहीं, बल्कि उनके अपने ही भीतर विराजमान ज्योति स्वरूप परमात्मा है। गुरु गीता के अनुसार, गुरु ही वह प्रकाश है जो जीव के 'मोह' के बंधन को काट देता है।

'ब्रह्मज्ञान' की इस शाश्वत अनुभूति के बाद ही जीव की वास्तविक भक्ति शुरू होती है। जब साधक अपने भीतर उस दिव्य प्रकाश का साक्षात्कार कर लेता है, तो उसके हृदय की गाँठें खुल जाती हैं और सारे संशय मिट जाते हैं– "भिद्यते हृदयग्रन्थिश्छिद्यन्ते सर्वसंशयाः"। मुण्डकोपनिषद् स्पष्ट करता है कि यह ज्ञान केवल तर्क या बुद्धि से नहीं मिलता, बल्कि 'सत्य' के साक्षात्कार से मिलता है। दिव्य दृष्टि प्राप्त होने पर मनुष्य यह अनुभव करता है कि वह फल खाने वाला दुखी पक्षी नहीं है, बल्कि वह तो वही अनंत चेतन तत्व है जो सदा से मुक्त है।

निष्कर्षतः मुण्डकोपनिषद् का यह प्रसंग आज के आधुनिक 'संजय' के लिए एक चेतावनी और समाधान दोनों है। हम सूचनाओं के फल खाने में इतने व्यस्त हैं कि अपने

भीतर बैठे उस 'साक्षी परमात्मा' को भूल गए हैं। जब तक हम एक पूर्ण सतगुरु की शरण लेकर अपने भीतर उस दिव्य ज्योति का दर्शन नहीं करते, तब तक हम संसार के सुख-दुख के चक्र में फँसे रहेंगे। 'ब्रह्मज्ञान' ही वह दिव्य चक्षु है जो हमें यह अनुभव कराता है कि परमात्मा कहीं दूर नहीं, बल्कि हमारे ही घट के भीतर प्रकाशमान है। साक्षात्कार ही वह अंतिम सत्य है जो जीवन को सार्थकता और पूर्णता प्रदान करता है।

अध्याय 7: प्रश्नोपनिषद्

प्रश्नोपनिषद् और अजपा-जाप: प्राण के रहस्य से अनहद के साक्षात्कार तक

मानव अस्तित्व का आधार क्या है? वह कौन सी शक्ति है जो शरीर को जीवित रखती है और उसे परमात्मा से जोड़ती है? प्रश्नोपनिषद् में महर्षि पिप्पलाद छह ऋषियों को 'प्राण' और 'ओम्' के विज्ञान का रहस्य समझाते हैं। वे बताते हैं कि ब्रह्मांड और शरीर का मूल 'प्राण' है। लेकिन अध्यात्म का सबसे गहरा सत्य यह है कि हमारे भीतर एक निरंतर जाप चल रहा है, जिसे 'अजपा जाप' कहा जाता है। यह वह जाप है जिसे जिह्वा से नहीं किया जाता, बल्कि यह प्राणों की गति के साथ स्वतः घटित हो रहा है। ऋषि पिप्पलाद समझाते हैं कि ओम् का वह परम स्वरूप केवल 'सुनने' या 'पढ़ने' का विषय नहीं है, बल्कि भीतर के जगत में 'अनुभव' करने का विषय है।

इस कथा का वैज्ञानिक पक्ष यह है कि 'अजपा जाप' प्रत्येक मनुष्य के भीतर चौबीस घंटे चल रहा है, परंतु अज्ञान के कारण हमें वह सुनाई नहीं देता। जैसे महर्षि पिप्पलाद ने शिष्यों को एक वर्ष की तपस्या के बाद दीक्षा दी, वैसे ही गुरुदेव श्री आशुतोष महाराज जी समझाते हैं कि बिना 'ब्रह्मज्ञान' और गुरु की कृपा के, जीव इस सूक्ष्म ध्वनि (अनाहत नाद) को नहीं सुन सकता। गुरु ही वह वैज्ञानिक है जो हमारी सुरति (चेतना) को बाहरी शोर से हटाकर भीतर के उस 'ओम्' के गुंजन से जोड़ देता है।

(A meditating person with focus on the throat and heart area, symbolizing the breath based Ajapa-Japa and the sound of Om radiating from within.)

गुरु की भूमिका यहाँ 'ओम्' (Omkar) के वास्तविक बोध में स्पष्ट होती है। महर्षि पिप्पलाद समझाते हैं कि ओम् केवल एक अक्षर नहीं, बल्कि 'ब्रह्म' की ध्वनि है। जब एक पूर्ण सतगुरु शिष्य के 'दिव्य चक्षु' और आंतरिक कर्णों को जाग्रत करते हैं, तब शिष्य को ज्ञात होता है कि 'अजपा जाप' ही वास्तविक साधना है। यह जाप गुरु कृपा से ही भीतर के जगत में प्रकट होता है। बिना गुरु की दीक्षा के मनुष्य केवल शब्दों का उच्चारण करता रहता है (सूचना), परंतु दीक्षा के बाद वह उस 'अजपा' के संगीत में विलीन हो जाता है (साक्षात्कार)।

इस उपनिषद् का सबसे महत्वपूर्ण सूत्र है कि वह 'पुरुष' (परमात्मा) इसी शरीर के भीतर है - "इहैव अन्तःशरीरे स पुरुषो..."। जब गुरु 'ब्रह्मज्ञान' प्रदान करते हैं, तो शिष्य अनुभव करता है कि ओम् की वह ध्वनि और प्रकाश कहीं बाहर से नहीं आ रहे, बल्कि उसके अपने ही प्राणों का मूल आधार हैं। जैसे नदियाँ समुद्र में मिलकर अपना नाम-रूप त्याग देती हैं, वैसे ही अजपा जाप के माध्यम से साधक की

चेतना परमात्मा के विराट 'महाप्राण' में विलीन हो जाती है। यह साक्षात्कार ही 'अमृतत्व' है।

निष्कर्षतः, प्रश्नोपनिषद् हमें सिखाता है कि हम 'संजय' की तरह केवल सूचनाओं के ज्ञाता न बनें। असली सत्य तो 'अजपा जाप' है, जो गुरु कृपा से ही भीतर ज्ञात होता है। जब गुरु की शक्ति से भीतर 'दिव्य चक्षु' खुलते हैं और 'अनाहत नाद' गूँजता है, तभी जीवन के सारे प्रश्न समाप्त होते हैं। यह प्रत्यक्ष दर्शन ही वह अंतिम सत्य है जो मनुष्य को पूर्णता और आत्मिक शांति प्रदान करता है।

अध्याय 8: ऐतरेय उपनिषद्

ऐतरेय उपनिषद्: सृजन के रहस्य से प्रज्ञानं ब्रह्म (चेतना) के साक्षात्कार तक

सृष्टि के आरम्भ में क्या था? वह कौन है जिसने इस शरीर और ब्रह्मांड का निर्माण किया? ऐतरेय उपनिषद् इन मौलिक प्रश्नों का उत्तर देते हुए कहता है कि आरम्भ में केवल 'आत्मा' ही थी। उसने अपनी इच्छा से लोकों की रचना की और फिर स्वयं उन शरीरों में प्रवेश किया। इस उपनिषद् का सबसे क्रांतिकारी सत्य यह है कि परमात्मा बाहर किसी स्वर्ग में नहीं बैठा है, बल्कि वह हमारे शरीर के शीर्ष (मस्तिष्क) के माध्यम से भीतर प्रविष्ट हुआ है। ऋषि ऐतरेय समझाते हैं कि वह 'ब्रह्म' ही हमारी आँखों में देखने वाला, कानों में सुनने वाला और मन में सोचने वाला मूल तत्व है।

इस उपनिषद् का महावाक्य है - "प्रज्ञानं ब्रह्म" (शुद्ध चेतना ही ब्रह्म है)। लेकिन इस चेतना का बोध केवल पढ़ने

या सुनने (सूचना) से नहीं होता। जैसे संजय महाभारत के दृश्यों को 'देख' तो रहा था पर 'अनुभव' नहीं कर पा रहा था, वैसे ही एक साधारण मनुष्य ईश्वर के बारे में सुनता तो है पर उसे 'जानता' नहीं। ऋषि ऐतरेय स्पष्ट करते हैं कि उस 'प्रज्ञान' (चेतना) का साक्षात्कार गुरु द्वारा प्रदत्त 'ब्रह्मज्ञान' से ही संभव है। जब गुरु कृपा से 'दिव्य चक्षु' खुलते हैं, तब मनुष्य यह देख पाता है कि वह शरीर नहीं, बल्कि वह विराट चेतन सत्ता है जो समस्त जगत का आधार है।

अध्यात्म का एक गुप्त रहस्य यह है कि हमारे भीतर 'अजपा जाप' और 'अनाहत नाद' के रूप में परमात्मा की उपस्थिति निरंतर विद्यमान है। गुरुदेव श्री आशुतोष महाराज जी अक्सर कहते हैं कि गुरु ही वह शक्ति है जो हमारी बिखरी हुई चेतना को समेटकर भीतर के उस 'महा-प्रकाश' से जोड़ देती है। ऐतरेय उपनिषद् के अनुसार, जब साधक गुरु की शरण में जाता है, तो उसे ज्ञात होता है कि भीतर जो 'प्रकाश' है, वही ब्रह्मांड का मूल है। बिना गुरु की कृपा के, मनुष्य 'स्वप्न' और 'जाग्रत' अवस्था के भ्रम में भटकता रहता है,

परंतु गुरु उसे 'तुरीय' (परम चेतना) की अवस्था का साक्षात्कार करा देते हैं।

इस उपनिषद् का मुख्य संदेश यह है कि जब जीव अपने वास्तविक स्वरूप को 'देख' लेता है, तो वह जन्म-मरण के चक्र से मुक्त हो जाता है। जैसे नचिकेता ने यमराज से और श्वेतकेतु ने आरुणि से ज्ञान पाया, वैसे ही ऐतरेय ऋषि का साधक अनुभव करता है कि वह 'प्रज्ञान' ही सत्य है। गुरु कृपा से जब भीतर 'अजपा जाप' और दिव्य ज्योति प्रकट होती है, तो जीव को अपने 'पूर्ण स्वरूप' का साक्षात्कार होता है। यही वह क्षण है जहाँ से 'असल भक्ति' का शुभारम्भ होता है, क्योंकि अब भक्त ईश्वर को केवल मानता नहीं, बल्कि साक्षात देखता है।

निष्कर्षतः, ऐतरेय उपनिषद् हमें 'संजय' की सूचनात्मक दृष्टि से ऊपर उठकर 'प्रज्ञान' (चेतना) के साक्षात्कार का मार्ग दिखाता है। ईश्वर दर्शन कोई कोरी कल्पना नहीं, बल्कि एक जीवंत सत्य है जो गुरु द्वारा प्रदत्त 'दिव्य दृष्टि' से संभव है। जब मनुष्य अपने भीतर उस शाश्वत

चेतना को पहचान लेता है, तभी जीवन की सार्थकता सिद्‌ध होती है। साक्षात्कार ही वह परम शांति है जो मनुष्य को अमरता प्रदान करती है।

अध्याय 9: केन उपनिषद्

केन उपनिषद्: मन के संचालक से 'ब्रह्म' के साक्षात्कार तक

"वह कौन है जिसकी इच्छा से मन अपने विषयों की ओर दौड़ता है? वह कौन है जो प्राणों को गति देता है और आँखों-कानों को शक्ति प्रदान करता है?" केन उपनिषद् इन्हीं मौलिक प्रश्नों (केन = किसके द्वारा) से आरम्भ होता है। ऋषि समझाते हैं कि जो आँखों से नहीं देखा जा सकता, बल्कि जिसके द्वारा आँखें देखती हैं; जो मन से नहीं सोचा जा सकता, बल्कि जिसके द्वारा मन सोचता है—वही 'ब्रह्म' है। यह उपनिषद् स्पष्ट करता है कि ईश्वर कोई बाहरी वस्तु नहीं है जिसे हम अपनी इंद्रियों से पकड़ सकें, बल्कि वह तो हमारी चेतना का भी मूल स्रोत है।

इस उपनिषद् का सबसे गहरा सत्य यह है कि जो व्यक्ति यह मानता है कि वह ब्रह्म को "जानता" है (बौद्धिक

रूप से), वह वास्तव में उसे नहीं जानता। क्योंकि ब्रह्म 'सूचना' (Information) नहीं, बल्कि 'साक्षात्कार' (Realization) का विषय है। ऋषि कहते हैं कि परमात्मा को वही जानता है जो उसे अपने प्रत्येक अनुभव (प्रतिबोध) में साक्षात देखता है। जैसे 'संजय' के पास महाभारत के दृश्यों की सूचना तो थी, पर अर्जुन की तरह उस दिव्य अनुभूति का अभाव था। ऋषि यहाँ स्पष्ट करते हैं कि गुरु की शरण में जाकर ही उस 'दिव्य चक्षु' का उद्घाटन संभव है, जिससे हम उस शक्ति को देख सकें जो हमारे भीतर 'अजपा-जाप' और 'प्राण' के रूप में थिरक रही है।

गुरु की अनिवार्यता को समझाने के लिए इस उपनिषद् में 'यक्ष और देवताओं' की एक कथा है। जब अग्नि, वायु और इंद्र को अपनी शक्ति पर अहंकार हो गया, तब ब्रह्म एक 'यक्ष' के रूप में प्रकट हुए। अग्नि एक तिनके को जला नहीं पाई और वायु उसे उड़ा नहीं पाई। तब इंद्र को बोध हुआ कि उनकी समस्त शक्तियाँ वास्तव में 'ब्रह्म' की ही देन हैं। यहाँ 'उमा' (दिव्य विद्या/गुरु शक्ति) प्रकट होती हैं और इंद्र को ब्रह्म का वास्तविक ज्ञान देती हैं। यह प्रसंग सिद्ध करता

है कि बिना गुरु शक्ति के, बड़ी-बड़ी शक्तियाँ और शास्त्र-ज्ञान भी व्यर्थ हैं। गुरु ही वह मार्गदर्शक है जो हमें यह बोध कराता है कि हमारे भीतर की ज्योति ही ब्रह्मांड का आधार है।

अध्यात्म का विज्ञान कहता है कि जैसे बिजली कौंधती है (विद्युतो व्यद्युतदा), वैसे ही गुरु की कृपा से साधक के अंतर्जगत में ब्रह्म का प्रकाश अचानक प्रकट होता है। इस 'क्षणमात्र' के साक्षात्कार के बाद ही जीव की 'असल भक्ति' शुरू होती है। गुरुदेव श्री आशुतोष महाराज जी अक्सर इसी पद्धति की चर्चा करते हैं कि जब गुरु 'ब्रह्मज्ञान' प्रदान करते हैं, तो मनुष्य अपनी आँखों को बंद करके उस परम प्रकाश को भीतर साक्षात देखता है। केन उपनिषद् के अनुसार, जिसने इसी जन्म में उस सत्य को देख लिया, उसका जीवन सार्थक है, अन्यथा महान विनाश (महती विनष्टिः) है।

निष्कर्षतः, केन उपनिषद् हमें 'संजय' की सतही दृष्टि से ऊपर उठाकर उस 'मूल शक्ति' के साक्षात्कार का मार्ग दिखाता है जो हमारे अस्तित्व का आधार है। ईश्वर को केवल

तर्कों से नहीं, बल्कि गुरु द्वारा प्रदत्त 'दिव्य दृष्टि' से भीतर देखना ही धर्म का वास्तविक लक्ष्य है। जब भीतर उस 'अजपा-जाप' और दिव्य प्रकाश की अनुभूति होती है, तभी मनुष्य अहंकार से मुक्त होकर पूर्ण शांति को प्राप्त करता है। साक्षात्कार ही वह अमृत है जो जीव को अमरता प्रदान करता है।

अध्याय 10: बृहदारण्यक उपनिषद्

बृहदारण्यक उपनिषद्: अज्ञान के अन्धकार से आत्म-ज्योति के साक्षात्कार तक

"असतो मा सद्गमय, तमसो मा ज्योतिर्गमय, मृत्योर्मा अमृतं गमय" (मुझे असत्य से सत्य की ओर ले चलो, अन्धकार से प्रकाश की ओर ले चलो और मृत्यु से अमरत्व की ओर ले चलो)। बृहदारण्यक उपनिषद् का यह सुप्रसिद्ध प्रार्थना मंत्र ही अध्यात्म का संपूर्ण सार है। ऋषि याज्ञवल्क्य इस उपनिषद् में राजा जनक और अपनी पत्नी मैत्रेयी को वह ज्ञान प्रदान करते हैं, जो मनुष्य को समस्त भौतिक बंधनों से मुक्त कर देता है। ऋषि स्पष्ट करते हैं कि इस संसार में जो कुछ भी हमें प्रिय लगता है, वह वास्तव में उस 'आत्मा' के कारण ही प्रिय है जो हमारे भीतर निवास करती है।

इस उपनिषद् का एक महान वैज्ञानिक प्रसंग राजा जनक और ऋषि याज्ञवल्क्य के बीच 'प्रकाश' को लेकर है।

राजा जनक पूछते हैं - "हे ऋषि! जब सूर्य डूब जाता है, चंद्रमा अस्त हो जाता है और अग्नि बुझ जाती है, तब मनुष्य किस प्रकाश के सहारे कार्य करता है?" ऋषि उत्तर देते हैं - "तब शब्द (ध्वनि) ही उसका प्रकाश होता है।" जनक फिर पूछते हैं - "और जब शब्द भी शांत हो जाता है, तब मनुष्य किसके सहारे चलता है?" तब याज्ञवल्क्य कहते हैं - "आत्मकैवास्य ज्योतिर्भवति" अर्थात् तब 'आत्मा' ही उसकी ज्योति (प्रकाश) होती है। यह प्रसंग सिद्ध करता है कि हमारी आँखों के पीछे एक और प्रकाश है, जिसे 'दिव्य चक्षु' के बिना नहीं देखा जा सकता।

ऋषि याज्ञवल्क्य समझाते हैं कि यह आत्म-ज्योति ही 'ब्रह्म' है, और इसका साक्षात्कार गुरु कृपा के बिना संभव नहीं है। इस उपनिषद् का महावाक्य है - "अहं ब्रह्मास्मि" (मैं ही ब्रह्म हूँ)। लेकिन यह केवल कहने की बात (सूचना) नहीं है। जैसे 'संजय' केवल बाहर की घटनाओं का वर्णन कर रहे थे, वैसे ही एक साधारण मनुष्य केवल शब्दों में कहता है कि "मैं ब्रह्म हूँ"। परंतु वास्तविक 'साक्षात्कार' तब होता है जब गुरु 'ब्रह्मज्ञान' की दीक्षा देते हैं। गुरु की शक्ति से जब

भीतर 'अजपा-जाप' और 'अनाहत नाद' गूँजता है, तब साधक साक्षात अनुभव करता है कि जो ज्योति सूर्य और चंद्रमा में है, वही ज्योति उसके अपने भीतर भी जल रही है।

गुरु की अनिवार्यता पर यह उपनिषद् बल देता है कि "आत्मा वा अरे द्रष्टव्यः श्रोतव्यो मन्तव्यो निदिध्यासितव्यः" (आत्मा ही देखने योग्य है, सुनने योग्य है, मनन करने योग्य है और ध्यान करने योग्य है)। यहाँ 'देखने योग्य' (द्रष्टव्यः) शब्द का अर्थ ही 'साक्षात्कार' है। गुरुदेव श्री आशुतोष महाराज जी अक्सर इसी वैदिक पद्धति को रेखांकित करते हैं कि ईश्वर कोई कल्पना नहीं, बल्कि एक 'दृश्य' है जिसे भीतर देखा जाता है। जब गुरु की कृपा से मनुष्य अपने भीतर उस शाश्वत प्रकाश को देख लेता है, तभी उसकी 'असल भक्ति' शुरू होती है। तब वह जान पाता है कि वह शरीर नहीं, बल्कि साक्षात परमात्मा का अंश है।

निष्कर्षतः, बृहदारण्यक उपनिषद् हमें 'संजय' की सीमित सूचनात्मक दृष्टि से ऊपर उठाकर उस 'आत्म-ज्योति' के दर्शन का मार्ग दिखाता है जो कभी अस्त नहीं होती। ईश्वर

को भीतर देखना ही अंधकार से प्रकाश की ओर जाने का वास्तविक अर्थ है। जब गुरु द्वारा प्रदत्त 'दिव्य दृष्टि' से हम अपने भीतर उस 'अहं ब्रह्मास्मि' के सत्य को प्रत्यक्ष देख लेते हैं, तभी जीवन से मृत्यु का भय समाप्त होता है। साक्षात्कार ही वह अमृत है जो जीव को दुखों से मुक्त कर पूर्णता प्रदान करता है।

अध्याय 11: माण्डूक्य उपनिषद्

माण्डूक्य उपनिषद्: ओम् के रहस्यों से तुरीय (परम चेतना) के साक्षात्कार तक

मानव चेतना किन स्तरों पर कार्य करती है? वह कौन सी अवस्था है जहाँ दुःख और द्वैत का अंत हो जाता है? माण्डूक्य उपनिषद् इन प्रश्नों का उत्तर 'ओम्' (AUM) के वैज्ञानिक विश्लेषण के माध्यम से देता है। ऋषि उद्घोष करते हैं कि यह सम्पूर्ण जगत 'ओम्' ही है। जो बीत चुका, जो वर्तमान है और जो भविष्य में होगा, वह सब ओम्कार है। परंतु ओम् केवल एक शब्द नहीं, बल्कि चेतना की वह यात्रा है जो जाग्रत, स्वप्न और सुषुप्ति (गहरी नींद) से परे 'तुरीय' अवस्था तक ले जाती है।

इस उपनिषद् का महावाक्य है - "अयमात्मा ब्रह्म" (यह आत्मा ही ब्रह्म है)। ऋषि समझाते हैं कि आत्मा के चार चरण हैं। पहला चरण जाग्रत अवस्था है जहाँ हम बाहरी

संसार को देखते हैं; दूसरा स्वप्न है जहाँ हम भीतर के मानसिक संसार को देखते हैं; तीसरा सुषुप्ति है जहाँ कोई इच्छा या स्वप्न नहीं रहता। परंतु चौथा चरण, जिसे 'तुरीय' कहा गया है, वही आत्मा का वास्तविक स्वरूप है। यह 'तुरीय' अवस्था ही वह शांत, शिव और अद्वैत तत्व है जिसे पाने के बाद कुछ पाना शेष नहीं रहता।

ऋषि स्पष्ट करते हैं कि इस 'तुरीय' अवस्था का साक्षात्कार केवल 'सूचना' (Information) से संभव नहीं है। जैसे 'संजय' केवल जाग्रत अवस्था की घटनाओं को देख रहे थे, परंतु अर्जुन ने 'तुरीय' के उस परम प्रकाश का अनुभव किया। इस अवस्था तक पहुँचने के लिए गुरु की अनिवार्य भूमिका होती है। गुरु ही वह वैज्ञानिक है जो 'ब्रह्मज्ञान' की पद्धति से साधक की चेतना को शरीर और मन के स्तर से ऊपर उठाकर उस परम तत्व से जोड़ देता है। गुरु कृपा से जब भीतर 'अजपा-जाप' और 'दिव्य ज्योति' प्रकट होती है, तब साधक ओम् के वास्तविक स्वरूप (अमात्र) को 'देख' पाता है।

गुरुदेव श्री आशुतोष महाराज जी अक्सर इसी चतुर्थ अवस्था (तुरीय) की चर्चा करते हैं कि यह कोई मानसिक कल्पना नहीं, बल्कि एक 'साक्षात्कार' है। जब गुरु 'दिव्य चक्षु' का उद्घाटन करते हैं, तब मनुष्य अनुभव करता है कि 'ओम्' की वह अनहद ध्वनि (अनाहत नाद) उसके भीतर निरंतर गूँज रही है। यही वह क्षण है जहाँ 'अयमात्मा ब्रह्म' एक जीवंत अनुभूति बन जाता है। इस दर्शन के बाद ही साधक की 'असल भक्ति' शुरू होती है, क्योंकि अब वह परमात्मा को अपनी आत्मा के रूप में साक्षात अनुभव करता है।

निष्कर्षतः माण्डूक्य उपनिषद् हमें सिखाता है कि हम केवल जाग्रत संसार के 'संजय' न बने रहें, बल्कि गुरु की शरण लेकर 'तुरीय' के द्रष्टा बनें। ईश्वर को भीतर देखना ही समस्त दुखों का अंत है। जब गुरु द्वारा प्रदत्त 'दिव्य दृष्टि' से हम ओम्कार के उस शांत और अद्वैत स्वरूप का दर्शन कर लेते हैं, तभी जीवन की पूर्णता सिद्ध होती है। साक्षात्कार ही वह अमृत है जो जीव को अमरत्व और परम शांति प्रदान करता है।

अध्याय 12: तैत्तिरीय उपनिषद्

तैत्तिरीय उपनिषद्: पंच-कोशों के भेदन से 'आनंद' के साक्षात्कार तक

मनुष्य का वास्तविक स्वरूप क्या है? क्या वह केवल मांस और हड्डियों का पुतला है, या इसके पीछे कोई दिव्य सत्ता है? तैत्तिरीय उपनिषद् इस रहस्य को 'पंच-कोश' के विज्ञान से स्पष्ट करता है। ऋषि समझाते हैं कि आत्मा पांच परतों (कोशों) में छिपी है: अन्नमय (शरीर), प्राणमय (ऊर्जा), मनोमय (मन), विज्ञानमय (बुद्धि) और अंत में आनंदमय (परम शांति)। संसार का हर जीव सुख खोज रहा है, पर वह सुख केवल बाहरी परतों तक सीमित है। ऋषि वरुण अपने पुत्र भृगु को समझाते हैं कि "आनंद" ही ब्रह्म है, क्योंकि आनंद से ही सब उत्पन्न होते हैं और अंत में उसी में विलीन हो जाते हैं।

इस उपनिषद् का मुख्य उद्घोष है - "रसो वै सः" (वह परमात्मा स्वयं रस/आनंद स्वरूप है)। परंतु इस आनंद का अनुभव इंद्रियों या सूचनाओं से नहीं हो सकता। जैसे 'संजय' के पास युद्ध की समस्त सूचनाएं थीं, परंतु वह 'अन्नमय' और 'मनोमय' स्तर पर ही था, इसलिए वह दुखी था। दूसरी ओर, अर्जुन ने कृष्ण की कृपा से उन परतों को भेदकर उस 'आनंदमय' ब्रह्म का साक्षात्कार किया। ऋषि स्पष्ट करते हैं कि गुरु की शरण में जाकर ही इन कोशों को पार कर उस अंतर्मन की ज्योति को देखा जा सकता है।

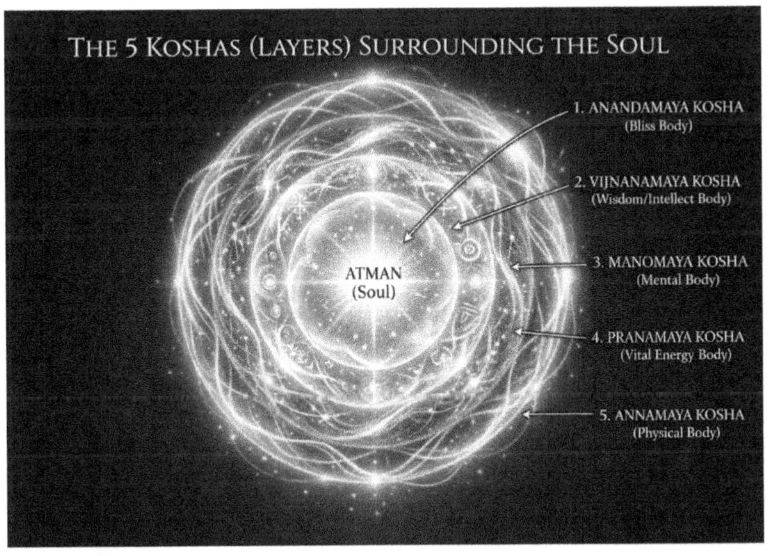

(The 5 layers (Koshas) surrounding the soul, like a radiant light at the centre protected by layers of energy, mind, and body.)

गुरु की अनिवार्यता पर यह उपनिषद् कहता है कि ब्रह्म का ज्ञान प्राप्त करना कोई कोरी कल्पना नहीं है। जब गुरु 'ब्रह्मज्ञान' की दीक्षा देते हैं, तो वे साधक को 'विज्ञानमय' (बुद्धि) से 'आनंदमय' (आत्मा) की ओर ले जाते हैं। गुरु ही वह शक्ति है जो भीतर चल रहे 'अजपा-जाप' की डोर पकड़ाकर साधक को हृदय-गुहा के उस गुप्त स्थान तक पहुँचाती है जहाँ प्रकाश ही प्रकाश है। गुरुदेव श्री आशुतोष महाराज जी अक्सर इसी पद्धति को समझाते हैं कि जब गुरु 'दिव्य चक्षु' का उद्घाटन करते हैं, तभी मनुष्य जान पाता है कि जिस शांति को वह बाहर खोज रहा था, वह उसके अपने ही केंद्र में 'प्रकाश' के रूप में विद्यमान है।

इस उपनिषद् का एक और महत्वपूर्ण सत्य है - "यतो वाचो निवर्तन्ते अप्राप्य मनसा सह" (जहाँ से वाणी और मन उसे पाए बिना ही लौट आते हैं)। इसका अर्थ है कि ईश्वर तर्क या शब्दों का विषय नहीं, बल्कि प्रत्यक्ष दर्शन का विषय है। जब गुरु की कृपा से भीतर 'अनाहत नाद' गूँजता है और दिव्य ज्योति प्रकट होती है, तब साधक 'भय' से मुक्त हो जाता है। यही वह क्षण है जहाँ से जीव की 'असल भक्ति'

शुरू होती है, क्योंकि अब वह आनंद को किसी वस्तु में नहीं, बल्कि स्वयं के भीतर साक्षात देखता है।

निष्कर्षतः तैत्तिरीय उपनिषद् हमें सिखाता है कि हम शरीर और मन की परतों में उलझे हुए 'संजय' न बनें, बल्कि भृगु की तरह गुरु-सानिध्य में 'आनंद' के खोजी बनें। ईश्वर दर्शन ही जीवन का परम आनंद है। जब गुरु द्वारा प्रदत्त 'दिव्य दृष्टि' से हम अपने भीतर उस 'रस स्वरूप' परमात्मा का अनुभव कर लेते हैं, तभी जीवन के सारे संघर्ष समाप्त होते हैं। साक्षात्कार ही वह अमृत है जो मनुष्य को पूर्ण तृप्ति और शाश्वत सुख प्रदान करता है।

अध्याय 13: ईशावास्य उपनिषद्

ईशावास्य उपनिषद्: जगत के कण-कण में व्याप्त 'प्रकाश' का साक्षात्कार

क्या ईश्वर इस संसार से अलग कहीं दूर आकाश में रहता है? ईशावास्य उपनिषद् इस धारणा को पहले ही मंत्र में स्पष्ट कर देता है - "ईशावास्यमिदं सर्वं यत्किञ्च जगत्यां जगत्" (इस गतिशील जगत में जो कुछ भी है, वह सब ईश्वर से व्याप्त है)। यह उपनिषद् सिखाता है कि हम जिस संसार को देख रहे हैं, वह केवल भौतिक पदार्थ नहीं है, बल्कि उस परम चेतना का ही विस्तार है। ऋषि कहते हैं कि इस सत्य को जानकर 'त्यागपूर्वक भोग' (तेन त्यक्तेन भुञ्जीथाः) करो। परंतु प्रश्न यह है कि जो ईश्वर सर्वत्र व्याप्त है, वह हमें दिखाई क्यों नहीं देता?

ऋषि इसका उत्तर देते हुए कहते हैं कि सत्य का मुख 'हिरण्मय पात्र' (सोने जैसे चमकीले ढक्कन) से ढका हुआ है

- "हिरण्मयेन पात्रेण सत्यस्यापिहितं मुखम्"। यह स्वर्ण पात्र हमारी बुद्धि का अहंकार और संसार का आकर्षण है। जैसे 'संजय' के पास युद्ध की समस्त सूचनाएँ और वैभव था, पर वह मोह के स्वर्ण पात्र के कारण कृष्ण के विराट स्वरूप को नहीं देख सका। ऋषि प्रार्थना करते हैं - "हे पूषन्! उस ढक्कन को हटा दो, ताकि मैं 'सत्य' को देख सकूँ।" यह प्रार्थना सिद्ध करती है कि ईश्वर को 'देखना' ही अध्यात्म का चरम लक्ष्य है।

(A brilliant golden sun (symbolizing the Hiranmaya Patra) being unveiled to reveal a serene, divine eye or light, representing the removal of the veil of ignorance.)

इस उपनिषद् में गुरु की भूमिका उस 'सूर्य' के समान है जो अज्ञान के परदे को हटा देता है। गुरु ही वह मार्गदर्शक है जो 'ब्रह्मज्ञान' की दीक्षा देकर साधक को उस पारलौकिक प्रकाश का दर्शन कराता है। ऋषि कहते हैं - "हे सूर्य! अपनी किरणों को समेट लो, ताकि मैं तुम्हारे उस अत्यंत कल्याणकारी रूप को देख सकूँ" - "यत्ते रूपं कल्याणतमं तत्ते पश्यामि"। यहाँ 'पश्यामि' (मैं देखता हूँ) शब्द प्रत्यक्ष साक्षात्कार का प्रमाण है। गुरु कृपा से जब भीतर 'अजपा-जाप' की डोर सक्रिय होती है और 'दिव्य चक्षु' खुलते हैं, तब साधक अनुभव करता है कि जो परमात्मा सूर्य के मंडल में है, वही मेरे भीतर भी है (योऽसावसौ पुरुषः सोऽहमस्मि)।

अध्यात्म का विज्ञान कहता है कि जो विद्या (ईश्वर ज्ञान) और अविद्या (संसार कर्म) दोनों को साथ लेकर चलता है, वही मृत्यु को पार कर अमरत्व प्राप्त करता है। गुरुदेव श्री आशुतोष महाराज जी अक्सर इसी वैदिक सत्य को समझाते हैं कि ईश्वर को मानना केवल एक सूचना है, परंतु उसे कण-कण में साक्षात देखना ही 'दर्शन' है। जब गुरु की शक्ति से भीतर 'अनाहत नाद' गूँजता है, तब साधक को बोध

होता है कि वह अकेला नहीं है, बल्कि ईश्वर उसके रोम-रोम में प्रकाशमान है। यही वह क्षण है जहाँ से 'असल भक्ति' शुरू होती है।

निष्कर्षतः ईशावास्य उपनिषद् हमें 'संजय' की सीमित सूचनात्मक दृष्टि से मुक्त कर 'ऋषि' की दिव्य दृष्टि प्रदान करता है। ईश्वर को संसार से अलग नहीं, बल्कि संसार के भीतर साक्षात देखना ही धर्म का वास्तविक अर्थ है। जब गुरु द्वारा प्रदत्त 'दिव्य दृष्टि' से हम उस 'हिरण्मय पात्र' को हटाकर भीतर के सत्य का दर्शन कर लेते हैं, तभी जीवन की पूर्णता सिद्ध होती है। साक्षात्कार ही वह अमृत है जो जीव को मोह के बंधनों से मुक्त कर शाश्वत शांति प्रदान करता है।

अध्याय 14: कौषीतकि उपनिषद्

कौषीतकि उपनिषद्: प्राण से प्रज्ञा तक और ब्रह्म-साक्षात्कार की पराकाष्ठा

मानव शरीर में वह कौन सी शक्ति है जो सर्वोत्तम है? कौषीतकि उपनिषद् में राजा प्रतर्दन और इंद्र (जो यहाँ ज्ञान के प्रतीक हैं) के संवाद के माध्यम से इस रहस्य को सुलझाया गया है। इंद्र कहते हैं - "प्राणो अस्मि प्रज्ञात्मा" अर्थात् "मैं प्राण हूँ और मैं ही प्रज्ञा (दिव्य बुद्धि) हूँ।" यह उपनिषद् स्पष्ट करता है कि हमारा जीवन केवल सांस लेना नहीं है, बल्कि उस चेतना का अनुभव करना है जो इन सांसों को चला रही है। ऋषि समझाते हैं कि जब तक शरीर में 'प्राण' है, तब तक ही जीवन है, और वह प्राण ही वास्तव में 'ब्रह्म' है।

इस उपनिषद् का सबसे गहरा वैज्ञानिक पक्ष यह है कि 'प्राण' और 'प्रज्ञा' (Consciousness) दोनों एक ही हैं।

जैसे 'संजय' के पास देखने की शक्ति तो थी, पर बिना दिव्य प्रज्ञा के वह कृष्ण के तत्व को नहीं समझ पाया। ऋषि कहते हैं कि वाणी, चक्षु, श्रोत्र और मन–ये सब प्राण के अधीन हैं। जब मनुष्य सोता है, तो उसकी वाणी प्राण में विलीन हो जाती है, उसकी आँखें प्राण में विलीन हो जाती हैं। यह प्रसंग सिद्‌ध करता है कि हमारे भीतर एक ऐसा 'केंद्र' है जहाँ सब कुछ एकाकार हो जाता है। उस केंद्र को जानना ही 'ब्रह्मज्ञान' है।

गुरु की भूमिका यहाँ 'प्रज्ञा' को जाग्रत करने में है। गुरु ही वह वैज्ञानिक है जो शिष्य को यह बोध कराता है कि इंद्रियों के विषयों को जानने के बजाय, उस 'दृष्टा' (देखने वाले) को जानो। ऋषि कहते हैं - "वाणी को मत जानो, बोलने वाले को जानो; रूप को मत जानो, देखने वाले को जानो।" यह 'देखने वाले' का साक्षात्कार ही गुरु कृपा से संभव है। जब गुरु 'दिव्य चक्षु' प्रदान करते हैं, तब साधक के भीतर 'अजपा-जाप' की ध्वनि गूँजती है और वह अनुभव करता है कि उसका प्राण उस 'महाप्राण' (परमात्मा) का ही अंश है।

अध्यात्म का विज्ञान कहता है कि जैसे रथ की नाभि में आरे (spokes) टिके होते हैं, वैसे ही भूत-मात्राएँ प्रज्ञा-मात्राओं पर और प्रज्ञा-मात्राएँ प्राण पर टिकी हैं। गुरुदेव श्री आशुतोष महाराज जी अक्सर इसी आंतरिक संतुलन की चर्चा करते हैं कि जब गुरु 'ब्रह्मज्ञान' की पद्धति से भीतर का द्वार खोलते हैं, तो मनुष्य को साक्षात प्रकाश का दर्शन होता है। कौषीतकि उपनिषद् के अनुसार, जो इस सत्य को 'देख' लेता है, वह पापों से मुक्त होकर आनंदमय लोक को प्राप्त होता है। यही वह क्षण है जहाँ से 'असल भक्ति' शुरू होती है।

निष्कर्षतः कौषीतकि उपनिषद् हमें 'संजय' की बाहरी सूचनात्मक दृष्टि से ऊपर उठाकर 'प्रज्ञा' के साक्षात्कार का मार्ग दिखाता है। ईश्वर को केवल प्राणों की गति में नहीं, बल्कि उन प्राणों के पीछे छिपी 'दिव्य चेतना' के रूप में भीतर देखना ही धर्म का वास्तविक लक्ष्य है। जब गुरु द्वारा प्रदत्त 'दिव्य दृष्टि' से हम उस आनंदमय, अजर और अमर तत्व का दर्शन कर लेते हैं, तभी जीवन की पूर्णता सिद्ध होती है।

साक्षात्कार ही वह दिव्य अनुभूति है जो मनुष्य को संसार के बंधनों से मुक्त कर शाश्वत शांति प्रदान करती है।

अध्याय 15: महानारायण उपनिषद्

महानारायण उपनिषद्: हृदय-कमल के भीतर 'दिव्य ज्योति' का साक्षात्कार

ब्रह्मांड का परम केंद्र कहाँ है? उस परमात्मा का निवास स्थान कहाँ है जिसे वेदों ने 'अणोरणीयान्' (अणु से भी सूक्ष्म) और 'महतो महीयान्' (महान से भी महान) कहा है? महानारायण उपनिषद् इस रहस्य का उद्घाटन करते हुए स्पष्ट करता है कि वह परमात्मा कहीं आकाश में नहीं, बल्कि मनुष्य के हृदय-कमल (दहर पुण्डरीक) के भीतर विराजमान है। ऋषि वर्णन करते हैं कि शरीर के मध्य में एक सूक्ष्म कोश है, जिसके भीतर एक छोटा सा 'आकाश' है। उस स्थान पर ध्यान लगाने से उस ज्योति का दर्शन होता है जो समस्त जगत को प्रकाशित करती है।

इस उपनिषद् का सबसे वैज्ञानिक मंत्र हृदय की संरचना और ज्योति के प्रकटीकरण को समझाता है -

"नीलतोयद-मध्यस्था विद्युल्लेखेव भास्वरा।" अर्थात् नीले मेघों के मध्य में बिजली की रेखा के समान वह ज्योति अत्यंत देदीप्यमान है। जैसे 'संजय' केवल बाहरी कुरुक्षेत्र को देख रहे थे, वैसे ही एक सामान्य मनुष्य केवल भौतिक हृदय (धड़कन) को जानता है। परंतु ऋषि स्पष्ट करते हैं कि गुरु द्वारा प्रदत्त 'ब्रह्मज्ञान' से जब 'दिव्य चक्षु' खुलते हैं, तब साधक को उस विद्युत जैसी चमक वाली ज्योति का साक्षात अनुभव होता है। यह ज्योति ही 'नारायण' है और यही आत्मा का वास्तविक स्वरूप है।

(The 'Dahara Akasha' - the subtle space within the heart where the Supreme Light resides.)

गुरु की अनिवार्यता पर यह उपनिषद् बल देता है कि बिना 'दीक्षा' और 'गुरु कृपा' के यह सूक्ष्म मार्ग ज्ञात नहीं होता। गुरु ही वह वैज्ञानिक है जो प्राणों की गति को नियंत्रित कर साधक को 'अजपा-जाप' के माध्यम से उस आंतरिक प्रकाश तक पहुँचाता है। महानारायण उपनिषद् के अनुसार, जो उस ज्योति को देख लेता है, वह 'परमं पदम्' (परम पद) को प्राप्त होता है। गुरुदेव श्री आशुतोष महाराज जी इसी वैदिक पद्धति को आधुनिक युग में प्रमाणित कर रहे हैं कि जब गुरु 'तीसरा नेत्र' जाग्रत करते हैं, तो मनुष्य अपनी आँखों को बंद करके उस 'तप्त-कार्तस्वर-प्रभं' (तपे हुए स्वर्ण जैसी आभा) वाली ज्योति को भीतर देखता है।

अध्यात्म का विज्ञान कहता है कि यह साक्षात्कार ही 'अमृतत्व' है। जब भीतर उस 'अनाहत नाद' का गुंजन होता है और दिव्य प्रकाश प्रकट होता है, तब साधक अनुभव करता है कि वह स्वयं उस प्रकाश का हिस्सा है - "सोऽहमस्मि"। यही वह क्षण है जहाँ से 'असल भक्ति' शुरू होती है। भक्त अब केवल कल्पना नहीं करता, बल्कि उस 'विश्वतश्चक्षुम्'

(सर्वव्यापी आँखों वाले) ईश्वर को अपने ही घट के भीतर साक्षात देखता है। इस दर्शन के बाद ही मनुष्य का 'अहंकार' भस्म होता है और वह पूर्ण शांति को प्राप्त होता है।

निष्कर्षतः महानारायण उपनिषद् हमें 'संजय' की सूचनात्मक दृष्टि से ऊपर उठाकर उस 'हृदय-ज्योति' के दर्शन का मार्ग दिखाता है जो बिजली की कौंध के समान सदा प्रकाशमान है। ईश्वर को केवल तर्कों में खोजना व्यर्थ है; उसे गुरु द्वारा प्रदत्त 'दिव्य दृष्टि' से हृदय-कमल के भीतर देखना ही धर्म का वास्तविक लक्ष्य है। जब गुरु की शक्ति से भीतर 'अजपा-जाप' और दिव्य ज्योति का संगम होता है, तभी जीवन की सार्थकता सिद्ध होती है। साक्षात्कार ही वह अंतिम सत्य है जो मनुष्य को अमरता और शाश्वत आनंद प्रदान करता है।

अध्याय 16: राजा परीक्षित पर गुरु की कृपा

परीक्षित का परम पद: कथा से साक्षात्कार और गुरु-हस्त की दिव्य शक्ति

श्रीमद्भागवत का सातवाँ दिन केवल एक कालखंड की समाप्ति नहीं, बल्कि एक जीवंत चमत्कार का साक्षी है। प्रसिद्ध संत डोंगरे जी महाराज इस प्रसंग की व्याख्या करते हुए एक अत्यंत गुप्त आध्यात्मिक रहस्य का उद्घाटन करते हैं। वे बताते हैं कि सात दिनों तक ज्ञान की अमृत वर्षा करने के बाद, जब शुकदेव मुनि ने देखा कि परीक्षित का मन संसार से पूरी तरह विरक्त हो चुका है, तब उन्होंने केवल उपदेशों पर विराम नहीं दिया, बल्कि उसे 'साक्षात्कार' की अंतिम अवस्था तक पहुँचाया। शुकदेव जी ने राजा परीक्षित के मस्तक (सहस्रार चक्र) पर अपना कर-कमल (हाथ) रखा और कहा– "हे राजन! अब तुम अपने नेत्र मूँद लो और अपना ध्यान उस ज्योति में लगाओ, जो मैं तुम्हारे भीतर प्रकट करने जा रहा हूँ।"

यह क्षण अध्यात्म के उस 'शक्तिपात' विज्ञान का प्रमाण है, जहाँ गुरु अपनी सामर्थ्य से शिष्य के भीतर के 'अंधकार' को हटाकर उसे 'परमात्मा' के साक्षात् दर्शन कराता है। राजा परीक्षित के लिए यह 'सूचना' (Information) के 'अनुभूति' (Experience) में बदलने का क्षण था। डोंगरे जी महाराज के अनुसार, गुरु का हाथ शिष्य के सिर पर होना वास्तव में 'दिव्य चक्षु' (तीसरे नेत्र) को जाग्रत करने की प्रक्रिया है। जैसे 'संजय' के पास केवल दूरदृष्टि थी, लेकिन परीक्षित को शुकदेव जी ने वह 'अंतर्दृष्टि' प्रदान की जिससे उन्होंने स्वयं को शरीर से पृथक एक 'प्रकाश स्वरूप' आत्मा के रूप में देखा। शुकदेव जी ने परीक्षित को आदेश दिया कि वे भीतर गूँज रहे 'अजपा-जाप' और 'अनाहत नाद' में लीन हो जाएँ। गुरु की इसी स्पर्श-दीक्षा से परीक्षित के भीतर वह ज्योति जाग्रत हुई, जो 'नीलतोयद-मध्यस्था' (बादलों के बीच बिजली) की भाँति देदीप्यमान थी।

इस घटना का वैज्ञानिक पक्ष यह है कि जब तक गुरु भीतर का द्वार नहीं खोलते, तब तक ईश्वर केवल एक 'कल्पना' या 'कहानी' बना रहता है। शुकदेव जी ने सात दिन

कथा सुनाई ताकि परीक्षित का 'मल' (पाप) और 'विक्षेप' (चंचलता) दूर हो जाए, और अंत में अपना हाथ उनके मस्तक पर रखकर उनके 'आवरण' (अज्ञान की परत) को हटा दिया। जैसे ही परीक्षित ने अपने भीतर उस 'आदित्यवर्णं' (सूर्य के समान प्रकाश) को देखा, उनके लिए 'तक्षक' नाग का भय स्वप्न के समान मिथ्या हो गया। उन्होंने अनुभव किया कि मृत्यु केवल वस्त्र बदलने के समान है, क्योंकि आत्मा तो अमर ज्योति है।

गुरुदेव श्री आशुतोष महाराज जी इसी सनातन पद्धति को रेखांकित करते हैं कि "ईश्वर दर्शन" आँखों को बंद करने के बाद शुरू होता है। डोंगरे जी द्वारा वर्णित यह 'गुरु-हस्त' की कृपा ही वह 'ब्रह्मज्ञान' है जो मनुष्य को 'संजय' की सूचनात्मक अवस्था से उठाकर 'शुकदेव' की साक्षात्कारी अवस्था में ले जाती है। जब गुरु की शक्ति से भीतर प्रकाश प्रकट होता है, तभी जीव की 'असल भक्ति' शुरू होती है, क्योंकि अब उसका विश्वास किसी के कहने पर नहीं, बल्कि 'स्वयं के देखने' (Self-Realization) पर आधारित है।

निष्कर्ष: राजा परीक्षित का प्रसंग हमें यह संदेश देता है कि आध्यात्मिक यात्रा का अंत 'सुनने' पर नहीं, बल्कि 'देखने' पर होता है। यदि शुकदेव जी जैसा गुरु मस्तक पर हाथ रखकर भीतर ज्योति प्रकट न करे, तो सात वर्षों की कथा भी मृत्यु का भय नहीं मिटा सकती। गुरु द्वारा प्रदत्त यह 'दिव्य दृष्टि' ही वह अंतिम सुरक्षा कवच है जो काल के मुख में भी जीव को अभय कर देता है। साक्षात्कार ही वह परम सत्य है जो जीव को ब्रह्म में विलीन कर अमरता प्रदान करता है।

अध्याय 17: शुकदेव मुनि की आध्यात्मिक यात्रा

श्री शुकदेव मुनि: तत्ववेत्ता गुरु और ब्रह्मज्ञान का वैज्ञानिक प्रकटीकरण

श्रीमद्भागवत पुराण के महानायक श्री शुकदेव जी का व्यक्तित्व अध्यात्म जगत में अद्वितीय है। वे 'परमहंस' अवस्था के प्रतीक हैं, लेकिन उनके जीवन का सबसे बड़ा रहस्य यह है कि जन्मजात ब्रह्मज्ञानी होने के बावजूद उन्हें एक 'देहधारी गुरु' (राजा जनक) की शरण लेनी पड़ी। महर्षि वेदव्यास के पुत्र शुकदेव जी जब गर्भ से ही ज्ञान लेकर निकले, तब भी पूर्णता के लिए उन्हें विदेह राजा जनक के पास भेजा गया। यह घटना सिद्ध करती है कि 'ब्रह्मज्ञान' का वास्तविक साक्षात्कार केवल एक 'जीवित तत्ववेत्ता गुरु' के सान्निध्य में ही संभव है।

1. राजा जनक से दीक्षा: गुरु-शिष्य परंपरा का आदर्श शुकदेव

जी को शास्त्रों का बोध था, पर उस बोध को 'साक्षात्कार' और 'स्थिरता' में बदलने के लिए उन्हें राजा जनक के पास जाना पड़ा। राजा जनक ने उनकी परीक्षा ली और अंततः उन्हें उस 'दिव्य चक्षु' (तीसरा नेत्र) का रहस्य प्रदान किया, जिससे शुकदेव जी की सुरति पूर्णतः ब्रह्म में लीन हो गई। यहीं से उन्होंने सीखा कि कैसे संसार के बीच रहकर भी 'विदेह' (शरीर के भाव से मुक्त) रहा जाता है। इसी शक्ति को लेकर वे आगे चलकर राजा परीक्षित के गुरु बने। डोंगरे जी महाराज के अनुसार, जो ज्ञान शुकदेव जी ने जनक से प्राप्त किया, वही उन्होंने परीक्षित को हस्तांतरित (Transfer) किया।

(Young Shukadeva bowing before King Janaka, representing the tradition of seeking a Guru for practical realization.)

2. सूचना बनाम साक्षात्कार: गुरु का वास्तविक दायित्व संसार में ज्ञान के दो स्तर हैं - 'परोक्ष' (सूचना) और 'अपरोक्ष' (साक्षात्कार)। राजा परीक्षित के पास मृत्यु के समय सूचनाओं की कमी नहीं थी, लेकिन वे काम नहीं आईं। शुकदेव जी ने सिद्ध किया कि गुरु का वास्तविक कार्य केवल शब्द बोलना नहीं, बल्कि 'भीतर ज्योति' प्रकट करना है। डोंगरे जी महाराज इस प्रसंग की व्याख्या करते हुए कहते हैं कि सात दिनों की कथा के बाद, शुकदेव जी ने परीक्षित के मस्तक पर अपना हाथ रखा और कहा - "हे राजन! अब तुम अपने नेत्र मूँद लो और अपना ध्यान उस ज्योति में लगाओ, जो मैं तुम्हारे भीतर प्रकट करने जा रहा हूँ।"

3. ब्रह्मज्ञान का विज्ञान और शक्तिपात: शुकदेव जी ने परीक्षित को उस 'अजपा-जाप' का रहस्य दिया जो श्वासों के साथ निरंतर चल रहा है। गुरु का हाथ शिष्य के सिर पर होना वास्तव में 'शक्तिपात' की प्रक्रिया है। इस शक्ति से शिष्य के भीतर 'अनाहत नाद' गूँजता है और 'दिव्य ज्योति' का दर्शन होता है। शुकदेव जी ने परीक्षित को सिखाया कि कैसे अपनी चेतना को उस आंतरिक 'प्रकाश' में लीन करना

है। यहीं 'संजय' (केवल सूचना देने वाला) समाप्त होता है और 'द्रष्टा' (साक्षात्कार करने वाला) जाग्रत होता है।

4. असल भक्ति: दर्शन के बाद की यात्रा: शुकदेव जी ने सिद्ध किया कि 'असल भक्ति' दर्शन के बाद शुरू होती है। जब तक गुरु भीतर का द्वार नहीं खोलते, तब तक ईश्वर केवल एक 'कल्पना' बना रहता है। राजा जनक से प्राप्त उसी 'ब्रह्मज्ञान' की शक्ति से शुकदेव जी ने परीक्षित को यह बोध करा दिया कि वे शरीर नहीं, बल्कि साक्षात् आत्मा हैं। परीक्षित ने स्वयं स्वीकार किया कि अब उन्हें मृत्यु का भय नहीं है, क्योंकि उन्होंने अपने भीतर उस 'अविनाशी ज्योति' का दर्शन कर लिया है।

अध्याय 18: गोपियों का अंतर्मन

ब्रज के गोप और गोपियाँ: प्रेम के आवरण में छिपे महान 'ब्रह्मज्ञानी'

श्रीमद्भागवत पुराण और गर्ग संहिता के गूढ़ प्रसंगों से यह स्पष्ट होता है कि ब्रज के गोप और गोपियाँ कोई साधारण सांसारिक जीव नहीं थे। वे पूर्व जन्मों के ऋषि-मुनि और श्रुतियाँ थीं, जिन्होंने भगवान के सान्निध्य के लिए गोकुल में अवतार लिया था। उनकी विशेषता यह थी कि वे श्री कृष्ण को केवल यशोदा-नंदन के रूप में बाहर से नहीं जानते थे, बल्कि गुरु कृपा से प्राप्त 'ब्रह्मज्ञान' के माध्यम से उन्हें अपने हृदय के भीतर 'परम ब्रह्म' के रूप में साक्षात् देखते थे। उनके लिए कृष्ण के साथ खेलना या दही बेचना केवल एक लौकिक क्रिया नहीं, बल्कि निरंतर चलने वाली एक समाधि थी।

1. अंतर्जगत का साक्षात्कार: बाहर और भीतर एक ही कृष्ण

गोपियों की भक्ति का आधार 'सूचना' (Information) नहीं,

बल्कि 'साक्षात्कार' (Realization) था। जैसे 'संजय' केवल बाहर की घटनाओं को देख रहे थे, वैसे ब्रजवासी नहीं थे। उन्हें वह 'दिव्य चक्षु' प्राप्त था जिससे वे यह जानते थे कि जो कृष्ण उनके सामने बाँसुरी बजा रहे हैं, वही उनके भीतर 'अजपा-जाप' और 'दिव्य ज्योति' के रूप में थिरक रहे हैं। जब कृष्ण ब्रज छोड़कर मथुरा चले गए, तब भी गोपियाँ दुखी होकर भी विचलित नहीं हुईं, क्योंकि उन्होंने गुरु कृपा से कृष्ण को अपने हृदय-कमल के भीतर स्थिर कर लिया था।

2. उद्धव का अहंकार और गोपियों का ब्रह्मज्ञान: जब कृष्ण ने परम ज्ञानी उद्धव को गोपियों को समझाने के लिए ब्रज भेजा, तो उद्धव का 'बौद्धिक ज्ञान' (Information) गोपियों के 'प्रत्यक्ष अनुभव' (Experience) के सामने फीका पड़ गया। उद्धव उन्हें निराकार ब्रह्म का उपदेश देना चाहते थे, परंतु गोपियों ने सिद्ध कर दिया कि वे उस निराकार को ही साकार रूप में अपने भीतर देख रही हैं। डोंगरे जी महाराज के अनुसार, गोपियों ने उद्धव को सिखाया कि वास्तविक ज्ञान वह नहीं जो किताबों में है, बल्कि वह है जो हृदय में 'प्रकाश' के रूप

में प्रकट होता है। ग्वालों और गोपियों के लिए कृष्ण 'घट-घट वासी' थे, जिसका दर्शन वे हर श्वास में करते थे।

3. अनाहत नाद और मुरली की तान: ग्वालों के लिए कृष्ण की मुरली केवल एक वाद्य यंत्र नहीं थी, बल्कि उनके भीतर गूँजने वाले 'अनाहत नाद' (Omkar) का बाहरी विस्तार थी। जब कृष्ण मुरली बजाते थे, तो ग्वालों की चेतना अनायास ही शरीर के भाव से ऊपर उठकर 'तुरीय' अवस्था में पहुँच जाती थी। गुरुदेव श्री आशुतोष महाराज जी अक्सर समझाते हैं कि ब्रजवासियों का प्रेम 'काम' नहीं, बल्कि 'निष्काम ब्रह्मज्ञान' था। उन्हें अपनी देह का बोध नहीं रहता था क्योंकि वे शुकदेव जी की भाँति आत्म-प्रकाश में लीन रहते थे। यही कारण था कि वे वन में हिंसक पशुओं के बीच भी अभय होकर विचरते थे।

4. कण-कण में दर्शन: प्रह्लाद जैसी दृष्टि भक्त प्रह्लाद की तरह, ब्रज के ग्वाले भी ईश्वर को कण-कण में देखते थे। वे कृष्ण के जूठे फल भी इसलिए खाते थे क्योंकि वे जानते थे कि 'प्रसाद' के रूप में वे उसी ब्रह्म शक्ति को ग्रहण कर रहे

हैं। उनके लिए माखन चुराना या मटकी फोड़ना 'ईशावास्य उपनिषद्' के सत्य का क्रियात्मक रूप था। वे जानते थे कि ब्रह्मांड का स्वामी उनके साथ खेल रहा है। उनका यह विश्वास किसी कहानी पर नहीं, बल्कि गुरु कृपा से प्राप्त उस 'शक्तिपात' पर टिका था, जिसने उनके भीतर के अंधकार को मिटाकर उन्हें 'कृष्ण-मय' कर दिया था।

निष्कर्ष: साक्षात्कार ही पूर्ण भक्ति है| ब्रज के गोप-गोपियों का जीवन संदेश देता है कि ईश्वर को 'मानना' केवल एक शुरुआत है, लेकिन उसे भीतर 'देखना' ही पूर्णता है। वे महान 'ब्रह्मज्ञानी' थे क्योंकि उन्होंने 'संजय' की सूचनात्मक दृष्टि को त्यागकर 'दिव्य दृष्टि' को अपनाया था। गुरु द्वारा प्रदत्त यह 'दिव्य प्रकाश' ही वह सूत्र था जिसने उन्हें नश्वर शरीर के मोह से मुक्त कर शाश्वत गोलोक की अनुभूति प्रदान की। साक्षात्कार ही वह अंतिम सत्य है जो भक्त और भगवान के बीच के भेद को मिटाकर उन्हें एक कर देता है।

अध्याय 19: गर्ग संहिता का प्रकाश

गर्ग संहिता के प्रकाश में ब्रजवासी: श्रुतियों और ऋषियों का 'ब्रह्म-साक्षात्कार'

गर्ग संहिता के 'गोलोक खण्ड' और 'वृंदावन खण्ड' के अनुसार, ब्रज के गोप-गोपियाँ कोई सामान्य ग्रामीण नहीं थे। गर्ग मुनि स्पष्ट करते हैं कि जब पूर्ण ब्रह्म श्री कृष्ण ने पृथ्वी पर अवतार लेने का निश्चय किया, तब उनके साथ उनकी 'हृदय-शक्ति' और 'ब्रह्मविद्या' के साक्षात् स्वरूपों ने भी अवतार लिया। इनमें से कुछ 'श्रुति-रूपा' (वेदों की ऋचाएँ) थीं, कुछ 'ऋषि-रूपा' (दंडकारण्य के तपस्वी ऋषि) थे और कुछ 'सिद्ध-रूपा' थे। इन सभी ने गुरु कृपा और कठिन तपस्या से वह 'ब्रह्मज्ञान' प्राप्त किया था, जिसके कारण वे कृष्ण को केवल बाहर ही नहीं, बल्कि अपने घट के भीतर भी साक्षात् अनुभव करते थे।

1. श्रुति-रूपा गोपियाँ: वेदों के 'साक्षात्कार' का साकार रूप गर्ग

संहिता के अनुसार, वेदों की ऋचाओं (Shrutis) ने जब भगवान के रसमय स्वरूप को जानने की इच्छा की, तो उन्हें ब्रज में गोपियों के रूप में जन्म मिला। वेदों का सार है - "तमेव विदित्वा" (उसे देख कर ही मृत्यु पार होती है)। इन गोपियों को वह 'दिव्य चक्षु' प्राप्त था, जिससे वे देख सकती थीं कि जो कृष्ण गौएँ चरा रहे हैं, वे ही वेदों द्वारा वर्णित 'अविनाशी तत्व' हैं। उनके लिए दही मथना या माखन निकालना केवल सांसारिक कार्य नहीं था, बल्कि 'अजपा-जाप' की लय में डूबी हुई एक निरंतर समाधि थी।

2. ऋषि-रूपा गोप और ग्वाले: तपस्या से 'तत्व दर्शन' तक

त्रेता युग में दंडकारण्य के जिन ऋषियों ने राम जी के सौंदर्य पर मुग्ध होकर उन्हें प्राप्त करना चाहा था, वे ही द्वापर में ग्वाले और गोपियाँ बने। इन ऋषियों के पास वर्षों का तप और 'ब्रह्मज्ञान' का संचित बल था। गर्ग संहिता वर्णन करती है कि जब श्री कृष्ण वन में कदम रखते थे, तो ग्वालों की चेतना देह-भाव से मुक्त होकर 'हृदय-गुहा' के प्रकाश में विलीन हो जाती थी। वे जानते थे कि कृष्ण के रूप में साक्षात् 'सत्य' उनके साथ खेल रहा है। उनके लिए 'कृष्ण' सूचना

(Information) नहीं, बल्कि एक जीवंत 'अनुभूति' (Realization) थे।

(The transition from ancient Sages in meditation to the same souls as Cowherds playing with Krishna in Braj, symbolizing the continuity of Brahmgyan.)

3. गोलोक की शक्ति और अंतर्जगत का प्रकाश: गर्ग संहिता में 'रास' का वर्णन कोई कामुक चेष्टा नहीं, बल्कि 'आत्मा' का 'परमात्मा' के साथ महा-मिलन है। यह वह अवस्था है

जहाँ 'अनाहत नाद' (मुरली की तान) और 'दिव्य ज्योति' (कृष्ण का स्वरूप) एक हो जाते हैं। ब्रजवासी जानते थे कि कृष्ण प्रत्येक जीव के 'हृदय' में उसी ज्योति के रूप में स्थित हैं जिसकी चर्चा उपनिषद करते हैं। गर्ग मुनि कहते हैं कि गोपियों के शरीर तो घर पर थे, लेकिन उनका मन कृष्ण की उस 'आंतरिक आभा' में लीन था, जो उन्होंने गुरु-शक्ति से अपने भीतर प्रकट की थी।

4. कण-कण में कृष्ण: 'सर्वं खल्विदं ब्रह्म' का प्रमाण गर्ग संहिता के अनुसार, जब कालिया नाग के दमन या गोवर्धन धारण जैसी लीलाएँ हुईं, तो ग्वालों और गोपियों का विश्वास विचलित नहीं हुआ। इसका कारण यह था कि वे कृष्ण को 'सर्वव्यापी' (Omnipresent) देखते थे। वे जानते थे कि 'ईशावास्य' के सिद्धांत के अनुसार कृष्ण ही जल, थल और अग्नि के भीतर प्रकाशमान हैं। डोंगरे जी महाराज के शब्दों में, उनकी भक्ति 'दर्शन' के बाद की भक्ति थी। उन्होंने श्री कृष्ण को 'परम प्रकाश' के रूप में अपने भीतर देख लिया था, इसलिए बाहरी चमत्कार उनके लिए स्वाभाविक थे।

निष्कर्ष: साक्षात्कार ही ब्रज की मूल शक्ति है| गर्ग संहिता सिद्ध करती है कि ब्रज के गोप-गोपियाँ श्रेष्ठ 'ब्रह्मज्ञानी' थे। उन्होंने 'संजय' की तरह केवल घटनाओं को सुना नहीं, बल्कि शुकदेव जी की तरह 'साक्षात्कार' किया था। गुरु कृपा द्वारा प्राप्त वह 'दिव्य दृष्टि' ही थी, जिसने उन्हें सांसारिक मोह-माया से मुक्त कर दिया और उन्हें 'कृष्ण-तत्व' के साथ एकाकार कर दिया। साक्षात्कार ही वह अमृत है जो जीव को 'भक्त' से 'मुक्त' की श्रेणी में खड़ा कर देता है।

अध्याय 20: गर्ग मुनि और नंद बाबा

गर्ग मुनि और नंद बाबा: पितृ-मोह से 'ब्रह्म-साक्षात्कार' तक की दिव्य यात्रा

गर्ग संहिता में एक अत्यंत मार्मिक और वैज्ञानिक प्रसंग आता है, जब यदुवंश के कुलगुरु गर्ग मुनि गुप्त रूप से नंद बाबा के यहाँ कृष्ण और बलराम के नामकरण संस्कार के लिए पहुँचते हैं। नंद बाबा कृष्ण को केवल अपना पुत्र मानते थे, जो कि 'पितृ-मोह' (अज्ञान) का प्रतीक था। गर्ग मुनि ने देखा कि नंद बाबा का प्रेम 'परोक्ष' है, वे केवल बाहरी रूप को देख रहे हैं। तब गर्ग मुनि ने नंद बाबा को उस 'ब्रह्मज्ञान' की दीक्षा दी, जिसने उनके 'पिता' के भाव को 'भक्त' और 'साक्षी' के भाव में बदल दिया। यह प्रसंग सिद्ध करता है कि बिना गुरु के तत्व-बोध के, साक्षात् ईश्वर के साथ रहते हुए भी मनुष्य उन्हें पहचान नहीं सकता।

1. गर्ग मुनि का तत्व-उपदेश: सूचना से परे का सत्य नंद

बाबा ने जब गर्ग मुनि का स्वागत किया, तब मुनि ने उन्हें स्पष्ट किया कि यह बालक कोई साधारण शिशु नहीं है। गर्ग संहिता के अनुसार, मुनि ने कहा - "नन्द! यह बालक साक्षात् 'नारायण' है, यह वही आदि-पुरुष है जिसकी स्तुति वेद करते हैं।" गर्ग मुनि ने नंद बाबा को वह 'परोक्ष ज्ञान' (Information) दिया कि कृष्ण ही 'ईशावास्य' के सिद्धांत के अनुसार कण-कण के स्वामी हैं। परंतु नंद बाबा की बुद्धि अभी भी संशय में थी, क्योंकि वे माया के आवरण में थे। तब गर्ग मुनि ने उन्हें वह 'दिव्य चक्षु' प्रदान किया, जिससे वे कृष्ण के वास्तविक स्वरूप को देख सकें।

2. अपरोक्ष साक्षात्कार: हृदय में कृष्ण का दर्शन गर्ग मुनि ने नंद बाबा को केवल सुनाया नहीं, बल्कि उनके भीतर उस 'अजपा-जाप' की डोर सक्रिय की, जो सीधे हृदय के 'प्रकाश' से जुड़ी थी। जैसे ही गर्ग मुनि की शक्ति नंद बाबा के भीतर उतरी, उन्हें अनुभव हुआ कि जो बालक उनके आँगन में खेल रहा है, वही उनके भीतर 'दिव्य ज्योति' के रूप में प्रकाशित है। डोंगरे जी महाराज के शब्दों में, गुरु के मस्तक पर हाथ रखते ही नंद बाबा का 'मोह' तिरोहित हो गया और उन्हें

'तत्व-दर्शन' प्राप्त हुआ। अब कृष्ण उनके लिए केवल पुत्र नहीं, बल्कि 'ब्रह्म' बन गए थे।

3. अनन्य भक्ति का उदय: दर्शन के बाद का विश्वास गर्ग संहिता वर्णन करती है कि इस दीक्षा के बाद नंद बाबा की भक्ति बदल गई। अब वे 'संजय' की तरह केवल कृष्ण की लीलाओं की सूचना रखने वाले नहीं थे, बल्कि वे 'शुकदेव' की तरह साक्षात् 'द्रष्टा' बन गए थे। जब भी कृष्ण पर कोई संकट आता (जैसे पूतना या तृणावर्त का वध), नंद बाबा विचलित नहीं होते थे, क्योंकि वे जानते थे कि 'सर्वशक्तिमान ब्रह्म' स्वयं उनके घर में है। यह अभय अवस्था केवल और केवल 'ब्रह्मज्ञान' के साक्षात्कार से ही संभव थी। गुरु की दीक्षा ने उन्हें यह बोध करा दिया कि कृष्ण उनसे कभी अलग हो ही नहीं सकते।

4. कण-कण में ब्रह्म का अनुभव: गर्ग मुनि की कृपा से नंद बाबा ने अनुभव किया कि कृष्ण केवल नंद-भवन में नहीं हैं, बल्कि वे चराचर जगत में व्याप्त हैं। 'गर्ग संहिता' के अनुसार,

नंद बाबा को हर वृक्ष, लता और गोकुल की मिट्टी में कृष्ण के ही 'अनाहत नाद' का गुंजन सुनाई देने लगा। यह वही 'ईशावास्य' सत्य था जिसे प्रह्लाद ने खंभे में देखा था। नंद बाबा का यह साक्षात्कार ही ब्रज की असली शक्ति थी। गुरु द्वारा प्रदत्त यह 'दिव्य दृष्टि' ही वह पारस पत्थर थी जिसने नंद बाबा के वात्सल्य प्रेम को 'दिव्य प्रेम' में बदल दिया।

निष्कर्ष: गुरु कृपा ही साक्षात्कार का मार्ग है| नंद बाबा और गर्ग मुनि का यह संवाद हमें सिखाता है कि साक्षात् भगवान के साथ रहते हुए भी हमें एक 'गुरु' की आवश्यकता होती है, जो हमारी आँखों से 'मोह' का पर्दा हटा सके। ईश्वर को 'पुत्र' या 'सखा' मानना प्रेम है, लेकिन उन्हें 'ब्रह्म' रूप में अपने भीतर देखना 'साक्षात्कार' है। गर्ग मुनि द्वारा दिया गया वह 'ब्रह्मज्ञान' ही वह प्रकाश है जो मनुष्य को नश्वर संसार से मुक्त कर अविनाशी तत्व में लीन कर देता है।

अध्याय 21: माता यशोदा की कथा

माता यशोदा: वात्सल्य के आँगन में 'विश्वरूप' का साक्षात् दर्शन

अध्यात्म के इतिहास में माता यशोदा का प्रसंग 'परोक्ष' (Information) और 'अपरोक्ष' (Realization) के बीच के अंतर को समझने का सबसे श्रेष्ठ उदाहरण है। माता यशोदा कृष्ण को अपना पुत्र मानती थीं, जो उनके प्रेम की पराकाष्ठा थी। परंतु 'गर्ग संहिता' के अनुसार, भगवान कृष्ण ने स्वयं अपनी माता को दो बार अपने मुख के भीतर संपूर्ण ब्रह्मांड का दर्शन कराकर यह सिद्ध किया कि जिसे वे अपनी गोद में खिला रही हैं, वही "सर्वं खल्विदं ब्रह्म" (सब कुछ ब्रह्म ही है) का मूल आधार है। यह प्रसंग स्पष्ट करता है कि ईश्वर को केवल 'स्नेह' से नहीं, बल्कि 'दिव्य चक्षु' के साक्षात्कार से जानना ही पूर्णता है।

1. मुख में ब्रह्मांड दर्शन: सूचना का साक्षात्कार में परिवर्तन

जब कृष्ण ने मिट्टी खाई और यशोदा मैया ने उन्हें मुँह खोलने को कहा, तब जो घटित हुआ वह कोई जादू नहीं, बल्कि 'ब्रह्मज्ञान' का क्रियात्मक प्रकटीकरण था। माता यशोदा ने कृष्ण के मुख में न केवल मिट्टी देखी, बल्कि चराचर जगत, दसों दिशाएँ, सूर्य, चंद्रमा, तारे और यहाँ तक कि स्वयं को और गोकुल को भी देखा। गर्ग संहिता के अनुसार, उस क्षण यशोदा मैया की चेतना 'अन्नमय' और 'मनोमय' कोशों को पार कर सीधे 'विज्ञानमय' कोश में पहुँच गई। उन्होंने साक्षात् देख लिया कि कृष्ण ही वह केंद्र हैं जिनसे पूरा ब्रह्मांड उत्पन्न होता है और जिनमें विलीन हो जाता है।

2. गर्ग मुनि की दीक्षा और यशोदा का बोध: यद्यपि यशोदा मैया को यह दर्शन कृष्ण की लीला से हुआ, परंतु इसके पीछे गर्ग मुनि द्वारा दी गई वह आध्यात्मिक पृष्ठभूमि थी जो उन्होंने नंद भवन में तैयार की थी। डोंगरे जी महाराज के अनुसार, जब गुरु मस्तक पर हाथ रखकर 'शक्तिपात' करते हैं, तभी बुद्धि इस योग्य होती है कि वह 'विश्वरूप' को झेल सके। यशोदा मैया को जब यह दर्शन हुआ, तो वे क्षण भर के लिए अपनी 'ममता' (माया) को भूल गईं और 'ब्रह्म' के

डर से कांपने लगीं। उन्हें अनुभव हुआ कि उनके भीतर गूँजने वाला 'अनाहत नाद' और उनके सामने खड़ा बालक एक ही तत्व हैं।

3. माया का आवरण और गुरु-तत्व की सूक्ष्मता: दर्शन के तुरंत बाद, भगवान ने अपनी 'वैष्णवी माया' से पुनः यशोदा मैया के बोध को ढक दिया ताकि वात्सल्य रस बना रहे। यह प्रसंग सिखाता है कि 'ब्रह्मज्ञान' प्राप्त होने के बाद भी संसार में व्यवहार करने के लिए गुरु की आज्ञा और मर्यादा आवश्यक है। यशोदा मैया 'संजय' की तरह केवल तटस्थ सूचना देने वाली नहीं थीं, बल्कि वे उस 'परम ज्योति' की प्रत्यक्ष द्रष्टा थीं। उन्होंने जान लिया था कि कृष्ण 'ईशावास्य' के सत्य के अनुसार उनके रोम-रोम में प्रकाशमान हैं। यही कारण था कि वे कृष्ण को दूध पिलाते समय भी अनजाने में उसी 'अजपा-जाप' की लय में रहती थीं।

4. कण-कण में दर्शन: वात्सल्य से अमरत्व तक गर्ग संहिता वर्णन करती है कि यशोदा मैया का प्रेम केवल एक बालक के प्रति नहीं था, बल्कि वह उस 'विश्वरूप' के प्रति था जिसे

उन्होंने अपने भीतर देख लिया था। प्रह्लाद की तरह, उन्हें भी गोकुल की मिट्टी और कृष्ण के चरणों की धूल में वही दिव्य प्रकाश दिखाई देता था। गुरुदेव श्री आशुतोष महाराज जी अक्सर इसी सत्य को समझाते हैं कि जब 'दिव्य चक्षु' खुलते हैं, तभी माता यशोदा की तरह मनुष्य को यह अनुभव होता है कि परमात्मा दूर नहीं, बल्कि उसके अत्यंत निकट– उसके अपने ही भीतर है।

निष्कर्ष: साक्षात्कार ही परम तृप्ति है| माता यशोदा का प्रसंग हमें सिखाता है कि ईश्वर को 'पुत्र' के रूप में पाना सौभाग्य है, लेकिन उन्हें 'ब्रह्म' के रूप में साक्षात् 'देखना' ही जीवन की सार्थकता है। गुरु कृपा से प्राप्त वह 'दिव्य दृष्टि' ही है जो हमें मोह के बंधनों से मुक्त कर 'दर्शन' के आनंद में डुबो देती है। यशोदा मैया का साक्षात्कार यह सिद्ध करता है कि ईश्वर 'सूचना' का विषय नहीं, बल्कि 'प्रत्यक्ष अनुभूति' का विषय है। जब हम अपने भीतर उस 'ज्योति' का दर्शन कर लेते हैं, तभी हम वास्तविक शांति और अमरत्व को प्राप्त होते हैं।

अध्याय 22: अक्रूर को दिव्य दर्शन

अक्रूर जी का यमुना-मंथन: जल के भीतर 'विशवरूप' और ब्रह्मज्ञान का साक्षात्कार

अध्यात्म के मार्ग पर अक्रूर जी का प्रसंग एक अत्यंत वैज्ञानिक सत्य को उद्‌घाटित करता है–कि ईश्वर को 'देखने' के लिए भौतिक नेत्रों की नहीं, बल्कि गुरु द्‌वारा प्रदान की गई 'दिव्य दृष्टि' की आवश्यकता होती है। अक्रूर जी, जो श्री कृष्ण के काका और एक परम ज्ञानी भक्त थे, उन्हें कृष्ण को मथुरा ले जाने का कार्य सौंपा गया था। मार्ग में यमुना तट पर जो घटना घटी, वह 'गर्ग संहिता' के अनुसार केवल एक चमत्कार नहीं, बल्कि 'ब्रह्मज्ञान' का प्रत्यक्ष क्रियात्मक परीक्षण था।

1. रथ और जल: सूचना और साक्षात्कार का द्‌वंद्‌व जब अक्रूर जी कृष्ण और बलराम को रथ पर बैठाकर मथुरा ले जा रहे थे, तब उनके मन में कृष्ण के प्रति श्रद्‌धा तो थी, लेकिन

वह 'परोक्ष' (Information) थी। वे जानते थे कि कृष्ण भगवान हैं, पर उन्होंने उस 'तत्व' को साक्षात् नहीं देखा था। यमुना में स्नान करते समय अक्रूर जी ने जो देखा, उसने उनके जीवन को बदल दिया। उन्होंने देखा कि जो कृष्ण रथ पर बैठे हैं, वही जल के भीतर शेषनाग की शय्या पर चतुर्भुज नारायण के रूप में स्थित हैं। यह दृश्य सिद्ध करता है कि कृष्ण "सर्वव्यापी" हैं - वे बाहर भी हैं और भीतर भी।

(Akrura submerged in the Yamuna river, witnessing the magnificent four-armed Vishnu and the cosmic form within the water, while Krishna sits calmly in the chariot outside.)

2. दिव्य चक्षु का प्रकटीकरण: जल के भीतर का प्रकाश गर्ग संहिता के अनुसार, अक्रूर जी को जल के भीतर जो 'विश्वरूप' दिखाई दिया, वह उनकी भौतिक आँखों का विषय नहीं था। श्री कृष्ण ने उस क्षण अक्रूर जी के 'दिव्य चक्षु' (तीसरे नेत्र) को जाग्रत कर दिया था। डोंगरे जी महाराज के अनुसार, जब तक गुरु 'शक्तिपात' नहीं करता, तब तक मनुष्य को जल में केवल जल और पत्थर में केवल पत्थर दिखता है। अक्रूर जी ने देखा कि संपूर्ण ब्रह्मांड, सूर्य, चंद्रमा और देवता उस ज्योतिर्मय पुरुष में विलीन हो रहे हैं। यह वही 'आदित्यवर्णं' प्रकाश था जिसका वर्णन श्वेताश्वतर उपनिषद् में मिलता है।

3. अजपा-जाप और अनाहत नाद की अनुभूति: अक्रूर जी ने जब जल के भीतर उस दिव्य स्वरूप को देखा, तो वे स्तब्ध रह गए। उन्होंने अनुभव किया कि उनके भीतर और बाहर एक ही 'अनाहत नाद' गूँज रहा है। गुरुदेव श्री आशुतोष महाराज जी अक्सर समझाते हैं कि वास्तविक 'तीर्थ' शरीर के भीतर है। अक्रूर जी के लिए यमुना का जल एक 'माध्यम' बन गया जिससे उन्होंने अपने भीतर के 'ब्रह्म-प्रकाश' का

साक्षात्कार किया। उन्होंने जान लिया कि कृष्ण 'ईशावास्य' के सत्य के अनुसार जल के प्रत्येक कण में व्याप्त हैं।

4. असल भक्ति: संदेह का अंत और दर्शन की पूर्णता अक्रूर जी जब जल से बाहर आए, तो कृष्ण ने मुस्कराकर पूछा - "काका! आपने जल में क्या देखा?" अक्रूर जी ने गद्गद होकर उत्तर दिया - "प्रभो! जो कुछ भी अद्भुत इस संसार में है, वह सब तो आपमें ही है।" यह उत्तर एक 'ज्ञानी' का नहीं, बल्कि एक 'साक्षात्कारी' का था। 'संजय' की तरह अक्रूर जी अब केवल घटना के वक्ता नहीं रहे, बल्कि वे 'द्रष्टा' बन गए। उनका 'मोह' और 'संशय' पूरी तरह नष्ट हो गया। उन्हें बोध हो गया कि कृष्ण को रथ पर बैठाकर ले जाना केवल एक लीला है, वास्तव में तो पूरा ब्रह्मांड कृष्ण में ही स्थित है।

निष्कर्ष: साक्षात्कार ही परम सत्य है| अक्रूर जी का यह प्रसंग हमें सिखाता है कि परमात्मा को केवल बाहर खोजने से बात नहीं बनेगी। जब तक गुरु कृपा से हमारे भीतर का 'यमुना-मंथन' नहीं होता और हमें वह 'दिव्य दृष्टि' प्राप्त

नहीं होती, तब तक हम कृष्ण को केवल एक 'ऐतिहासिक पात्र' (Information) ही मानते रहेंगे। अक्रूर जी की तरह अपने भीतर उस 'ज्योति' का दर्शन करना ही धर्म का वास्तविक लक्ष्य है। साक्षात्कार ही वह अमृत है जो मनुष्य को संसार के बंधनों से मुक्त कर परम पद तक पहुँचा देता है।

अध्याय 23: कुब्जा का उद्धार

कुब्जा का उद्धार: आंतरिक टेढ़ेपन का अंत और ब्रह्मज्ञान का 'ऋजु' मार्ग

मथुरा की गलियों में श्री कृष्ण और कुब्जा (त्रिवक्रा) का मिलन अध्यात्म के एक गहरे वैज्ञानिक सत्य को दर्शाता है। कुब्जा, जिसके शरीर में तीन टेढ़ेपन (कूबड़) थे, वास्तव में उस जीव का प्रतीक है जो 'त्रिविध ताप' (आधिभौतिक, आधिदैविक और आध्यात्मिक) और तीन गुणों (सतो, रजो, तमो) के बंधन में जकड़ा हुआ है। 'गर्ग संहिता' के अनुसार, कृष्ण ने उसे केवल शारीरिक सुंदरता प्रदान नहीं की, बल्कि उसके 'ब्रह्मज्ञान' के सोए हुए केंद्रों को जाग्रत कर उसे 'साक्षात्कार' की अवस्था तक पहुँचाया।

1. त्रिवक्रता और सुषुम्णा नाड़ी का विज्ञान: कुब्जा के शरीर के तीन मोड़ - गर्दन, पीठ और कमर - मनुष्य की इड़ा, पिंगला और सुषुम्णा नाड़ियों के असंतुलन और अविद्या के

आवरण के प्रतीक हैं। जब तक जीव का 'अहंकार' और 'विकार' रहता है, उसकी चेतना 'टेढ़ी' (वक्र) रहती है। कृष्ण ने कुब्जा के पैरों के अंगूठों को अपने पैरों से दबाया और उसकी ठुड्डी को ऊपर उठाया। यह क्रिया वास्तव में 'शक्तिपात' की एक विधि है, जिससे गुरु शिष्य की चेतना को मूलाधार से उठाकर सीधे 'आज्ञा चक्र' (तीसरे नेत्र) पर प्रतिष्ठित कर देता है।

2. स्पर्श-दीक्षा और दिव्य चक्षु का उद्घाटन: गर्ग संहिता के अनुसार, कृष्ण के स्पर्श मात्र से कुब्जा की रीढ़ की हड्डी सीधी हो गई और वह एक सुंदर स्त्री में बदल गई। परंतु यहाँ 'सुंदरता' का अर्थ आंतरिक दिव्यता से है। उस क्षण कृष्ण ने उसके 'दिव्य चक्षु' खोल दिए। डोंगरे जी महाराज के अनुसार, कुब्जा ने अनुभव किया कि जो सामने खड़ा है, वही उसके भीतर 'दिव्य ज्योति' के रूप में प्रकाशित है। अब वह 'संजय' की तरह केवल कृष्ण के बारे में सुनने वाली नहीं थी, बल्कि वह शुकदेव जी की तरह प्रत्यक्ष 'द्रष्टा' बन गई थी।

3. अनन्य भक्ति: सूचना से साक्षात्कार तक कुब्जा पहले केवल 'कंस' के लिए चंदन ले जाने वाली एक दासी थी। उसके

पास कृष्ण के बारे में 'सूचना' (Information) तो थी, लेकिन 'साक्षात्कार' (Realization) नहीं था। कृष्ण के स्पर्श ने उसके भीतर 'अजपा-जाप' और 'अनाहत नाद' को जाग्रत कर दिया। वह इतनी 'कृष्ण-मय' हो गई कि उसने भगवान का पीताम्बर पकड़ लिया और उन्हें अपने घर चलने का निमंत्रण दिया। यह निमंत्रण केवल भौतिक नहीं था, बल्कि अपनी अंतरात्मा में परमात्मा को सदा के लिए बसा लेने की पुकार थी।

4. कण-कण में दर्शन और आत्म-बोध: गर्ग संहिता के 'मथुरा खण्ड' में वर्णन है कि कुब्जा का हृदय अब 'ब्रह्म-भाव' में स्थित हो गया था। प्रह्लाद की भाँति, उसे भी अब मथुरा की गलियों में केवल कंस का भय नहीं, बल्कि कृष्ण का प्रकाश दिखाई देने लगा। गुरुदेव श्री आशुतोष महाराज जी अक्सर समझाते हैं कि "ऋजु" (सीधा) होना ही योग है। जब चेतना 'सुषुम्णा' में प्रवाहित होती है, तभी जीव को 'ब्रह्मज्ञान' का वास्तविक अनुभव होता है। कुब्जा का सीधा होना उसके 'अज्ञान' के समाप्त होने और 'आत्म-बोध' के उदय होने का प्रतीक है।

निष्कर्ष: साक्षात्कार ही पूर्ण रूपांतरण है| कुब्जा का प्रसंग हमें सिखाता है कि हम सब भी अपने विचारों और कर्मों में 'टेढ़े' (वक्र) हैं। जब तक हमें कृष्ण जैसा गुरु नहीं मिलता, जो हमारे मस्तक पर हाथ रखकर या अपनी शक्ति से हमें सीधा न कर दे, तब तक हम 'ब्रह्म' को नहीं देख सकते। ईश्वर को 'मानना' सूचना है, लेकिन कृष्ण के स्पर्श से उसे अपने भीतर 'देखना' ही 'साक्षात्कार' है। यही वह अंतिम सत्य है जो मनुष्य के समस्त विकारों को मिटाकर उसे 'परम सुंदरी' (शुद्ध आत्मा) में बदल देता है।

अध्याय 24: भक्त प्रह्लाद

भक्त प्रह्लाद: घट-घट वासी ईश्वर का द्रष्टा और ब्रह्मज्ञान की शक्ति

श्रीमद्भागवत पुराण में भक्त प्रह्लाद की कथा 'प्रत्यक्ष साक्षात्कार' और 'गुरु-दीक्षा' के विज्ञान का जीवंत प्रमाण है। प्रह्लाद ने अपने जीवन से सिद्ध किया कि ईश्वर केवल वैकुण्ठ में सीमित नहीं है, बल्कि वह "ईशावास्यमिदं सर्वं" के सिद्धांत के अनुसार सृष्टि के प्रत्येक अणु में व्याप्त है। प्रह्लाद की यह यात्रा केवल जन्मजात संस्कारों की नहीं, बल्कि गुरु द्वारा प्रदत्त उस प्रकाश की है जो अज्ञान के अंधकार को जड़ से मिटा देता है।

1. गर्भ में बोध और जन्म के बाद दीक्षा: गुरु-मिलन की अनिवार्यता प्रह्लाद के जीवन का सबसे महत्वपूर्ण पक्ष उनकी गुरु-शरण है। जब वे अपनी माता कयाधू के गर्भ में थे, तब देवर्षि नारद ने उन्हें आत्म-ज्ञान का उपदेश दिया था। परंतु,

जैसे शुकदेव जी जन्मजात ब्रह्मज्ञानी होने के बाद भी पूर्णता के लिए राजा जनक की शरण में गए, वैसे ही प्रह्लाद के लिए भी जन्म के बाद गुरु का सान्निध्य अनिवार्य था। गर्भ का ज्ञान एक 'बीज' के समान था, लेकिन उसे 'वृक्ष' बनाने के लिए जन्म के बाद गुरु की प्रत्यक्ष उपस्थिति और दीक्षा की आवश्यकता पड़ी। गुरु नारद ने प्रह्लाद की चेतना को 'अजपा-जाप' और 'दिव्य ज्योति' के उस क्रियात्मक अनुभव से जोड़ा, जिसने उन्हें संसार के बीच रहकर भी निर्लिप्त रखा।

2. कण-कण में दर्शन: ईशावास्य उपनिषद् का व्यावहारिक स्वरूप ईशावास्य उपनिषद् कहता है कि यह संपूर्ण जगत ईश्वर से व्याप्त है। प्रह्लाद ने इस सत्य को केवल सुना नहीं था, बल्कि गुरु कृपा से इसे 'देखा' था। जब उनके पिता हिरण्यकशिपु ने पूछा– "कहाँ है तेरा ईश्वर? क्या वह इस खंभे में भी है?" तब प्रह्लाद ने पूरे आत्मविश्वास से कहा– "हाँ पिता जी, वह इस खंभे में भी है और मुझमें और आपमें भी है।" यह उत्तर वही दे सकता है जिसके पास 'दिव्य चक्षु' (तीसरा नेत्र) हो। प्रह्लाद के लिए वह खंभा केवल पत्थर नहीं

था, बल्कि गुरु द्वारा दी गई दृष्टि से उन्हें उस पत्थर के भीतर भी वही ज्योतिर्मय ईश्वर दिखाई दे रहा था।

3. शक्तिपात और अभय अवस्था: शुकदेव जी की भाँति प्रह्लाद के जीवन में भी गुरु-कृपा 'शक्तिपात' के रूप में उतरी। नारद मुनि द्वारा प्रदान किए गए 'ब्रह्मज्ञान' ने प्रह्लाद को देह-अध्यास (शरीर का मोह) से मुक्त कर दिया था। यही कारण था कि अग्नि, विष और हाथियों के प्रहार भी उन्हें विचलित नहीं कर सके। जब गुरु शिष्य के भीतर 'अनाहत नाद' और दिव्य प्रकाश प्रकट कर देते हैं, तब शिष्य 'संजय' की सूचनात्मक अवस्था से ऊपर उठकर 'द्रष्टा' बन जाता है। प्रह्लाद उस आंतरिक ज्योति में इतने गहरे डूबे थे कि उन्हें बाहरी कष्टों का आभास ही नहीं हुआ।

4. असल भक्ति: साक्षात्कार के बाद का अटूट विश्वास प्रह्लाद की भक्ति 'दर्शन' पर टिकी थी। डोंगरे जी महाराज के अनुसार, जब गुरु मस्तक पर हाथ रखकर भीतर ज्योति प्रकट करते हैं, तभी 'अनन्य भक्ति' का उदय होता है। प्रह्लाद को ईश्वर को 'मानने' के लिए किसी तर्क की आवश्यकता नहीं थी,

क्योंकि वे उसे हर क्षण साक्षात् 'देख' रहे थे। भगवान नृसिंह का खंभे से प्रकट होना वास्तव में प्रह्लाद के उसी आंतरिक दर्शन का बाहरी प्रमाण था। यह कथा सिखाती है कि गुरु की दीक्षा वह पारस पत्थर है जो एक बालक को भी त्रिकालदर्शी महापुरुष बना देती है

अध्याय 25: कालिया नाग दमन

कालिया नाग दमन: मन के सौ विकारों का मर्दन और ब्रह्म-प्रकाश का उदय

यमुना के विषैले दह में कालिया नाग का दमन केवल एक वीरता की गाथा नहीं है, बल्कि यह मानव मनोविज्ञान और अध्यात्म के गहरे अंतर्संबंधों का प्रकटीकरण है। कालिया नाग के सौ फन मनुष्य के भीतर स्थित अनगिनत कामनाओं, क्रोध और 'अहंकार' के प्रतीक हैं, जिन्होंने जीवन रूपी यमुना को विषैला कर दिया है। 'गर्ग संहिता' के अनुसार, कृष्ण का उन फनों पर नृत्य करना वास्तव में 'ब्रह्मज्ञान' की वह प्रक्रिया है जिसमें गुरु शिष्य के 'अहंकार' को कुचलकर उसकी चेतना को 'परम प्रकाश' से जोड़ देता है।

1. सौ फन और कुण्डलिनी का रहस्य: कालिया के सौ फन उन विकारों को दर्शाते हैं जो आत्मा को घेरे हुए हैं। जब तक ये विकार जागृत हैं, जीव 'अविद्या' के विष से ग्रसित रहता

है। कृष्ण (जो कि पूर्ण गुरु और ब्रह्म के प्रतीक हैं) ने इन फनों पर प्रहार किया। यह आध्यात्मिक रूप से 'शक्तिपात' का संकेत है। जब गुरु शिष्य को दीक्षा देते हैं, तो वे अपनी शक्ति से शिष्य के 'मन' (नाग) को वश में करते हैं। जैसे ही कृष्ण के चरण कमलों का स्पर्श कालिया के मस्तक पर हुआ, उसका सारा विष (अज्ञान) समाप्त हो गया और वह निर्मल हो गया।

2. अनाहत नाद और दिव्य नृत्य: गर्ग संहिता वर्णन करती है कि जब कृष्ण नाग के फनों पर नृत्य कर रहे थे, तब ब्रह्मांड में अद्‌भुत 'अनाहत नाद' गूँज रहा था। यह नृत्य कोई साधारण क्रिया नहीं थी, बल्कि यह शरीर के भीतर स्थित 'षट-चक्रों' के भेदन की प्रक्रिया थी। डोंगरे जी महाराज के अनुसार, जब गुरु शिष्य के भीतर 'ब्रह्मज्ञान' प्रकट करते हैं, तो शिष्य को अपने ही घट के भीतर उस 'दिव्य संगीत' और 'प्रकाश' का अनुभव होता है। कालिया नाग का मस्तक झुकना इस बात का प्रमाण है कि 'बुद्‌धि' अब 'ब्रह्म' के अधीन हो गई है।

3. सूचना से साक्षात्कार: कालिया की पत्नियों की प्रार्थना जब कालिया की पत्नियों (नागपत्नियों) ने कृष्ण की स्तुति की, तो उनका ज्ञान 'परोक्ष' (Information) से 'अपरोक्ष' (Realization) की ओर बढ़ रहा था। उन्होंने जान लिया कि जो बालक उनके पति के फनों पर नृत्य कर रहा है, वही 'ईशावास्य' सत्य के अनुसार जल और थल का स्वामी है। 'संजय' की तरह केवल घटनाओं को देखना पर्याप्त नहीं था; कालिया के लिए वह साक्षात्कार का क्षण था। गुरुदेव श्री आशुतोष महाराज जी अक्सर समझाते हैं कि जब कृष्ण (ज्ञान) हमारे मन (नाग) पर आरूढ़ होते हैं, तभी जीवन की यमुना शुद्ध होती है और हमें 'दिव्य चक्षु' प्राप्त होते हैं।

4. कण-कण में दर्शन और अभय अवस्था: दमन के बाद कालिया नाग भयमुक्त होकर समुद्र की ओर चला गया। यह 'अभय' अवस्था केवल 'साक्षात्कार' के बाद ही आती है। प्रह्लाद की तरह कालिया ने भी अब जान लिया था कि वह 'विषाक्त जीव' नहीं, बल्कि उसी 'दिव्य ज्योति' का एक अंश है। गर्ग संहिता सिद्ध करती है कि कृष्ण का स्पर्श अशुद्ध को शुद्ध और पापी को साक्षात्कारी बना देता है। जब साधक अपने

भीतर उस 'अजपा-जाप' की डोर पकड़ लेता है, तो उसके भीतर का 'कालिया' (अहंकारी मन) शांत होकर परमात्मा का दास बन जाता है।

निष्कर्ष: साक्षात्कार ही वास्तविक दमन है| कालिया नाग दमन का संदेश स्पष्ट है - जब तक हमारे भीतर के 'अहंकार' के फन ऊँचे हैं, हम 'ब्रह्म' का अनुभव नहीं कर सकते। केवल गुरु द्वारा प्रदत्त 'ब्रह्मज्ञान' ही वह शक्ति है जो हमारे विकारों को कुचलकर हमें अपनी आत्मा का साक्षात् दर्शन करा सकती है। ईश्वर को बाहर खोजना सूचना है, लेकिन कृष्ण को अपने मन के फनों पर नचाना (वश में करना) और भीतर ज्योति देखना ही 'साक्षात्कार' है। यही वह अंतिम सत्य है जो संसार के विष को अमृत में बदल देता है।

अध्याय 26: प्रकृति में ब्रह्म का साक्षात्कार

गोवर्धन लीला: इंद्र के गर्व का मर्दन और प्रकृति में 'ब्रह्म-साक्षात्कार'

ब्रज की लीलाओं में गोवर्धन धारण की घटना 'परोक्ष ज्ञान' (Information) को 'अपरोक्ष साक्षात्कार' (Realization) में बदलने का सर्वोत्कृष्ट उदाहरण है। यह लीला सिद्ध करती है कि ईश्वर केवल स्वर्ग में रहने वाली कोई सत्ता नहीं है, बल्कि वह 'ईशावास्य' सत्य के अनुसार प्रकृति के कण-कण और पर्वत-शिलाओं में भी साक्षात् विद्यमान है। श्री कृष्ण ने इंद्र के 'बौद्धिक अहंकार' को चुनौती देकर ब्रजवासियों को यह बोध कराया कि वास्तविक पूजा केवल भयवश किया गया कर्मकांड नहीं, बल्कि उस तत्व का 'प्रत्यक्ष दर्शन' है जो संपूर्ण सृष्टि का आधार है।

1. इंद्र का गर्व और 'परोक्ष' ज्ञान का भ्रम: देवराज इंद्र को यह भ्रम था कि वे ही वर्षा के स्वामी हैं और उनकी पूजा

अनिवार्य है। यह 'अहंकार' का प्रतीक है। भगवान कृष्ण ने नंद बाबा और ग्वालों को समझाया कि हमें उस गोवर्धन की पूजा करनी चाहिए जो हमें प्रत्यक्ष फल दे रहा है। भगवान का संदेश था कि ईश्वर को केवल अदृश्य मानकर पूजा न करें, बल्कि उसे 'विश्वरूप' में अनुभव करें। गर्ग संहिता में श्री कृष्ण कहते हैं: "गोवर्धनो गिरिवरः साक्षाच्छ्रीपुरुषोत्तमः। पूजनीयो प्रयत्नेन सर्वकामफलप्रदः॥" (अर्थात्: यह श्रेष्ठ गोवर्धन पर्वत साक्षात् श्री पुरुषोत्तम ही है। यह समस्त कामनाओं का फल देने वाला है, अतः इसकी प्रयत्नपूर्वक पूजा करनी चाहिए।) जब कृष्ण ने स्वयं को 'गोवर्धन' के रूप में प्रकट कर बलि (भोग) ग्रहण किया, तब उन्होंने 'अद्वैत' के उस सत्य को प्रतिपादित किया जिसे ग्वालों ने पहली बार प्रत्यक्ष अनुभव किया।

2. पर्वत में 'ब्रह्म' का दर्शन: दिव्य चक्षु का विज्ञान जब कृष्ण ने गोवर्धन का रूप धारण किया, तब ब्रजवासियों को वह 'दिव्य चक्षु' (तीसरा नेत्र) प्राप्त हुआ जिससे उन्हें पत्थर की शिलाओं में भी 'परम ज्योति' के दर्शन हुए। यह क्षण उनके लिए 'शक्तिपात' के समान था। जैसे 'संजय' केवल

दिव्य दृष्टि से कुरुक्षेत्र देख रहे थे, वैसे ही ग्वालों ने देखा कि जिस पर्वत को वे बाहर देख रहे हैं, वही उनके भीतर 'दिव्य प्रकाश' के रूप में प्रकाशित है। गर्ग संहिता में इस अलौकिक दृश्य का वर्णन है: "सद्यो वैकुण्ठतां प्राप्तो गोवर्धनधरो गिरिः। सर्वलोकप्रदीप्तोऽसौ तेजसा स्वेन राजते॥" (अर्थात्: वह गोवर्धन पर्वत तत्क्षण साक्षात् वैकुण्ठ के समान दिव्य हो गया और अपने तेज से समस्त लोकों को प्रकाशित करने लगा।)

3. सात दिन की स्थिरता: 'अजपा-जाप' और आंतरिक योग

कृष्ण ने गोवर्धन पर्वत को सात दिनों तक अपनी कनिष्ठा उंगली पर धारण किया। यह 'सात दिन' मनुष्य के शरीर के सात चक्रों और जीवन की पूर्णता के प्रतीक हैं। मूसलाधार वर्षा के बीच भी ग्वाले भयभीत नहीं थे, क्योंकि वे कृष्ण के साथ उस 'अनाहत नाद' और आंतरिक शांति में स्थित हो गए थे जहाँ संसार का कोई भी तूफान (दुख) पहुँच नहीं सकता। जब पूर्ण गुरु 'ब्रह्मज्ञान' की छत्रछाया प्रदान करता है, तो शिष्य का मन पूर्णतः स्थिर हो जाता है। यह स्थिरता ही वास्तविक योग है।

4. इंद्र की शरणागति और साक्षात्कार: अंत में जब इंद्र का अहंकार टूटा, तो उन्होंने कृष्ण की स्तुति की। इंद्र ने स्वीकार किया कि वे केवल 'सूचना' (Information) के स्तर पर कृष्ण को जानते थे, लेकिन आज उन्हें 'साक्षात्कार' (Realization) हुआ है। गर्ग संहिता के 'गिरिराज खण्ड' में इंद्र कहते हैं: "त्वां ब्रह्म परमं साक्षात्प्रकृतेः परतः स्थितम्। द्रष्टुं मया न शक्यं त्वामृते ज्ञानदृशा विभो॥" (हे विभो! आप प्रकृति से परे साक्षात् परम ब्रह्म हैं। ज्ञान-दृष्टि (दिव्य दृष्टि) के बिना आपको देख पाना संभव नहीं है।) यह स्वीकारोक्ति ही वास्तविक 'ब्रह्मज्ञान' है, जहाँ जीव अपने संकुचित बोध को त्यागकर विराट तत्व में लीन हो जाता है।

निष्कर्ष: साक्षात्कार ही अभय का मार्ग है| गोवर्धन लीला का संदेश यह है कि जब मनुष्य अपने भीतर के 'गोवर्धन' (स्थिर प्रज्ञा) को जाग्रत कर लेता है, तो मानसिक वासनाओं की वर्षा उसका कुछ नहीं बिगाड़ सकती। ईश्वर को पत्थर में मानना 'सूचना' हो सकती है, लेकिन पर्वत में साक्षात् 'ब्रह्म' का दर्शन करना ही 'साक्षात्कार' है। यही वह अंतिम

सत्य है जो भक्त को प्रकृति के बंधनों से मुक्त कर अमृतत्व प्रदान करता है।

ABOUT THE AUTHOR

Anmol Setia

Anmol Setia was born on 29 July 2003 in Malout, a serene town in the Sri Muktsar Sahib district of Punjab, into the esteemed Setia family. From an early stage of his academic journey, while pursuing his higher secondary education in the non-medical stream, he was blessed to come under the divine refuge of his revered Guru, Ashutosh Maharaj Ji. He received sacred initiation (diksha) through His grace.

Balancing both spiritual pursuit and academic excellence, he completed his Bachelor's degree in Physics from Panjab University, Chandigarh. He is currently advancing his academic journey by pursuing a Master's degree in Physics at IIT Delhi.

Deeply inspired by the divine wisdom of his Guru, his life reflects a harmonious blend of scientific inquiry and spiritual awakening, which finds expression in his literary work The Divine Eye.

www.ingramcontent.com/pod-product-compliance
Lightning Source LLC
Chambersburg PA
CBHW051549130526
44974CB00022B/432

* 9 7 8 9 3 5 8 9 0 5 4 0 3 *